The Corporation

The Corporation:

Its History and Future

By

David Sarokin and

Jay Schulkin

Cambridge
Scholars
Publishing

The Corporation: Its History and Future

By David Sarokin and Jay Schulkin

This book first published 2020

Cambridge Scholars Publishing

Lady Stephenson Library, Newcastle upon Tyne, NE6 2PA, UK

British Library Cataloguing in Publication Data
A catalogue record for this book is available from the British Library

ISBN (10): 1-5275-4868-6
ISBN (13): 978-1-5275-4868-8

CONTENTS

ABOUT THIS BOOK

The world, it seems, has a love-hate relationship with corporations. Consumers line up for hours—days, even—for the latest iPhone, but recoil at reports that employees of an Apple contractor in China are leaping off factory roofs in despair over low salaries and harsh working conditions. We love our cars for the freedom they provide, their elegant lines and technological sophistication but worry about the automobile's contribution to smog and global warming, especially when we learn that Volkswagen has been rigging its emission tests. How cool is that we can search online for any piece of information on any topic and Google will find it almost instantly; but how disconcerting is it that Google is also collecting millions of gigabytes of data on the web habits of each of its billion-plus users. Love my new Nikes or the cute little Disney sweatshirt for my niece, but did those items come from some brutal sweatshop in Indonesia or a firetrap factory in Haiti?

Governments face similar contradictions regarding the corporations in their midst. On the one hand, corporations are recognized as engines of the economy, providers of employment and vital contributors to innovation. Corporations pay taxes on income and on transactions that are important sources of revenue for governments at all levels of operation. Nations the world over actively encourage corporate growth, partner with private firms, and busily engage corporate services. On occasion, corporations and governments are almost indistinguishable: the Saudi Aramco oil company essentially funds the nation of Saudi Arabia, for example.

At the same time, governments are just as energetically regulating company activities, fining corporate violations, breaking up—or threatening to break up—corporations that have become too large, too powerful, too influential for anyone's good. The Volkswagen tale is as good an example as any. The company deliberately rigged the software in their diesel engine cars to engage pollution controls during emission testing situations, but to turn off those same controls during ordinary driving conditions. As a result of these so-called "defeat devices", emissions testing results were so positive that Volkswagen received several "Clean Diesel" awards for outstanding technological achievement. But in reality, Volkswagen vehicles were emitting about 40 times more pollution on the road than they did in the testing laboratories. When researchers first identified the discrepancy, the results seemed so anomalous that they were convinced their testing equipment was faulty.

News of the subterfuge broke in 2015 and was met with widespread outrage. Investigations were begun in multiple countries. Lawsuits were filed. The corporation's stock price plunged as the extent of the deceit grew clear. Volkswagen's CEO was given the axe. In 2018, Germany took the step—rare for any country—to actually arrest Rupert Stadler, the CEO of Audi (a Volkswagen subsidiary) for his role in what came to be known as Dieselgate. Volkswagen was fined billions of dollars, committed billions more to retrofit the affected vehicles and compensate owners, and will pay out more billions as lawsuits are settled.

So how is the company faring in the face of all this adverse activity? Quite nicely, thank you. They managed to become the world's largest automotive manufacturer in 2016, overtaking Toyota for the top spot, and have held that position since. The company is profitable and has been every year but one since the scandal broke. The value of a share of Volkswagen stock, though not yet back to pre-scandal prices, has been climbing fairly steadily and is rated (ca. 2020) a Strong Buy by most analysts.

Governments intent on seeing Volkswagen punished for its misdeeds did not want to see the company crippled. In the U.S., the carmaker was fined $2.8 billion even though fines almost ten times that amount were permissible under the law. In Germany, where Volkswagen is headquartered, and in all the countries where the firm operates, legal actions seemed a kind of "tough love" designed to send a message: "We want to keep you around for a long, long time, so don't do this again!"

Such bureaucratic forbearance was not always the case and for several hundred years, the love-hate dialectic with corporations played out quite differently. Governments allowed corporations to exist only sparingly, with restrictions on their scope of operations and their overall lifespan. The small number of corporations permitted to operate were granted a temporary charter, a way of saying, in effect: "Let's give this venture ten or twenty years. We'll see how well it performs and what advantages it provides to society at large. If we're suitably impressed, we'll consider extending your charter. If not, you will cease to exist."

It doesn't work that way anymore. Corporations have become perpetual. Chartering a new corporation—once a rarity—is now as simple and as commonplace as opening a new bank account. Corporations are assumed to be a societal 'good' not for any specific outcome of corporate activities, but simply for existing and by existing, being an engine for economic growth.

At least, that's the "official" view held by governments, economists, think thanks and policy-makers. The public at large, though, is not so sure. Corporations featured in popular entertainment are almost always the bad guys: heartless, soulless megamonsters exploiting the masses, raping the environment, corrupting governments, invading privacies, unleashing diabolical technologies and generally bent on total domination. It's fiction, of course, but it's not an unfamiliar sentiment. Indeed, it's hard to bring to mind a modern film with a positive angle on big business. Villainous storylines notwithstanding, one truism about the depictions of corporations in popular fiction is that they wield enormous power in the modern world. It's a power that stems from several factors.

Money, of course, is central to corporate power. Money and power have always walked hand in hand. Such a large percentage of the world's wealth flows through corporate coffers that it's small wonder that individual companies can be as influential as individual nations, a theme we explore in several of the chapters ahead.

Money is not the sole route to power, however. As the saying goes, "Information is power." Corporations collect and manage huge swaths of information. It's not unusual for a company to massage data on hundreds of millions or even billions of people. Even when kept private, the information is used in increasingly intrusive ways. Keeping the information private, though, is turning out to be a challenge. Insecure corporate IT systems routinely result in harmful leaks of private information—*your* information—making public the passwords, emails, phone numbers, Social Security numbers, and online habits of much of the population of the planet. Another book of ours, *Missed Information*, looks at this aspect of the corporate world in detail, but we touch upon it here as well.

A third route to power comes from the world of ideas. Jesus of Nazareth, Martin Luther King, Mahatma Ghandi and Rosa Parks are powerful historical figures not for the wealth they accumulated or the data they managed, but for the power of their ideas, the inspiration of their actions, and the ability of their messages to resonate with so many people. Creative ideas of a different sort, from the likes of James Watt, Confucius, Albert Einstein, Susan B. Anthony and Michael Jackson, exercise a powerful influence as well.

Corporations engage in creative ideas that can be broadly and deeply influential. Certain products and services capture the public imagination, hence the long lines for iPhones or the popularity of previously unimagined peer-to-peer services like Uber and Airbnb. Product creativity exists behind the scenes as well, such as the corporate contributions to industry standards that underlie all our cell phones, USB connections and credit cards. Corporate creativity is hugely influential in our cultural milieu, influencing the foods we eat, the clothes we wear, the entertainment we watch, the music we hum to ourselves, and the ways in which we interact.

Corporate ideas—corporate ideology, if you will—also extends deeply into the political arena. Corporate executives sit at the table with presidents and prime ministers, heads of government agencies, elected representatives, newspaper editors, official task forces, non-profit organizations and anyone else in a position to influence public policies and make them more favorable to the world of business. They not only comment on drafts of laws, regulations, directives and treaties; they sometimes write them, a process facilitated by corporate contributions to select politicians and advocacy groups. None of this should come as a surprise.

Corporations have been in positions of great power for as long as the corporate model has existed. In their heyday, enterprises like the British East India Company and the Hudson Bay Company ran entire nations...or close to it. America's very first corporation, though a modest affair, was founded by two of the young country's preeminent power brokers, George Washington and James Madison. The reach of even a single large corporation, into millions of businesses and billions of people, is astounding.

Not everyone is comfortable with corporations amassing so much wealth and influence. We've mentioned popular movies already, but even serious works of non-fiction, several of them referenced in this book, expound on the dangers corporations pose to the democratic process. Thinkers as varied as Adam Smith, Thomas Jefferson and Bernie Sanders have warned of the dangers of corporate excess. The Progressive Era in American politics had a strong anti-corporate bent, one that resurfaces repeatedly in movements like Occupy Wall Street in the U.S. and some of the Green Party's agenda in Europe.

When we mentioned to a colleague that we were working on a book about corporations, their past and future, he commented grimly: "The future? Corporations win!" Perhaps they will. And "winning" could mean the sort of heartless, dystopian future that movie-makers (and our colleague, perhaps) envision. But it doesn't have to mean that. Corporations do unquestionable damage in the world, but they also provide so much that is needed or desirable. They produce goods, they produce bads. As authors, it strikes us as important to lay out our own orientation. Ours is not an anti-corporation work. We admire some of what the corporate world has accomplished, appreciate the give and take of the marketplace that allows some products and some firms to thrive and forces others to adapt or disappear, and are thankful for a growing economy that we are lucky enough to find ourselves in the midst of.

But we are mindful of the enormous wealth and influence wielded by corporations and with it, the enormous power to destroy, to corrupt, to rewrite the rules in their favor. We look to the past to understand why corporations came into being and how they emerged into their modern form. We explore the uneasy balance of corporations, governments, media and the many interests and concerns of the public. It's the general public, after all, that brings corporations into existence: the end consumer buying corporate products, the labor force powering corporate operations, and the communities, local and global, that interact with companies in so many different ways. We look to the future and wonder whether corporations will still exist a hundred years from now.

We trust you will find this of interest.

David Sarokin
Jay Schulkin

INTRODUCTION

We feel obliged to start with a mention of Antarctica as it's the only continent that does not appear anywhere else in this book about corporations. That may not surprise you. Outside of lots of ice, there's very little to attract a business to Antarctica: no roads, no cities, no subways, no stores, no Starbucks...no people! And a subtler absence—there are no corporations in Antarctica.

There are companies with a presence on the icy continent, firms that send employees or equipment to the handful of research stations or that provide transportation and communication services. But no corporations make Antarctica their home. Nor could they. This isn't a matter of the very limited market or the lack of infrastructure. There are no corporations because Antarctica has no government. It is instead governed—if that's the right term—by the consensus of individual countries that are party to various international treaties. The absence of a government, by necessity, means the absence of incorporated entities.

Corporations are creatures of governments, brought into being when governments decide their existence has merit, and, for much of history, dissolved when their benefits are no longer compelling. . It is kings and queens and parliaments and legislatures that create the legal framework for a corporation and these authorities have more or less unrestricted power to extend—or end—a corporation's existence. At least, that was the case for several centuries from the 1500's onward. The 20th and 21st centuries have seen a shift in the creation of corporations and the factors that can lead to a company's demise. The authority of modern governments to revoke a corporate charter is an open question.

An exploration of why corporations exist and the ways in which they operate certainly involves understanding what the incorporators hope to gain beyond that provided by a simple partnership or an informal collection of individuals. But understanding corporations also entails understanding governments. What do the powers-that-be—the kings and queens and parliaments and legislatures—hope to achieve by allowing, even

Figure Intro-1: A research station in Antarctica

encouraging, corporations to form in their midst?

Antarctica notwithstanding, we touch upon most of the world in various places in this book. England features prominently, as it can be thought to have brought the modern corporation into being. But our European coverage also includes Spain, France, Germany, Holland, Italy and elsewhere. In Asia, we touch on India, Japan, China and Korea. Other parts of the world—Ethiopia, South Africa, Canada, Mexico, Brazil, Australia—get attention as well, however briefly. We look at the meaning of *corporations* very broadly, spending a bit of text to examine corporations of all types, whether focused on business or the many other types of incorporated entities: towns, churches, non-profit organizations, schools, and so on. However, this is largely a book about the emergence of the almost-modern corporation in England and the explosive growth of business corporations in the United States.

The story of corporations is very much an American story, at least in the 19th and 20th centuries. The roots of the corporate form can be traced back to ancient Rome—or further—and corporations emerged as global powers in 17th century Europe. But the business corporation as it is familiar to us today is largely an American invention, one that emerged directly from another American invention, our peculiar form of representative government.

The division of government authority in the United States between federal and state governments had a profound influence on corporate activity in early America, and the division between branches of government made for a continual shaping and reshaping of corporate rights and responsibilities.

The impact of corporate growth in the US in the 19th century can be seen in a few numbers: in 1820, the GDP of Britain was three times the size of the GDP of the United States. By 1870, the UK economy had practically tripled in size while the US economy increased eight-fold, and the two were essentially equal. By 1913, the United States economy was more than double the size of Britain. The engine of this rapid growth in the U.S. was the emergence of the modern corporation. The US and the UK each had about 1,000 business corporations in 1800. By 1860, this number had grown to about 7,000 in Britain and 26,000 in the US. In the early 1900s, 60% of the world's business corporations made their home in America. US dominance remained solid throughout the 1900's, but globalization of the economy is rapidly changing the face of the corporate world, a topic we'll explore later in this book.

So why did corporations arise? Why did the United States play such an outsized role? And why are corporations so dominant today?

The reasons corporations came into being, the factors contributing to their dramatic growth and the societal response to both encourage and control corporations are the focus of this book. We begin in Chapter 1 by exploring some of the challenges of convening a group of people—any group, at any time in history—and looking at the role that corporations can play in addressing some of those problems, and then takes a more detailed look at the qualities and characteristics of corporations. The emergence of business corporations in quasi-modern form gets a detailed look in Chapter 2.

The corporate model in the United States occupies a good deal of the text in the middle of our book. Chapter 3 looks at incorporation in Europe and in early America, recognizing the similarities but focusing on the distinct situation in the colonies that called forth a different model of doing business. We visit with George Washington, James Madison and early entrepreneurs as they establish America's very first corporation. Corporations grew rapidly in the U.S., as did economic and societal problems associated with monopolies, Robber Barons, and what many saw as the soulless and increasingly dangerous dominance of big business. We look at the emergence of corporate regulation in Chapter 4 and consider, in Chapter 5, what it meant to operate a sizable and nearly global monopoly in the late 19th and early 20th century as compared with one of today's behemoths—Amazon.

The explosive growth of corporations coincided with an equally explosive growth in invention as tinkerers the world over learned to harness energy, create clever machinery and develop new processes of manufacturing. Once again, it was the peculiar institutions in the United States that led to a reinventing of the patent system itself. We look at the intersection of corporations and patents in Chapter 6.

As corporations became subject to increasingly stringent regulatory environments, they did not react with passive acceptance. Throughout history, businesses have pushed for maximum independence and for new ways to exercise power. In the modern world, that often meant turning to courts and legislatures and, most recently, international treaties as a means of securing additional rights, a topic we explore in Chapter 7.

We look too, to the future. What will the corporation of the next century look like? Will corporations even still exist, or will the purposes they have they served in the economies of the past few centuries be supplanted by new models of business, new social arrangements, or even by new technologies that render managerial decision-making obsolete? We examine the possibilities in Chapter 8.

CHAPTER 1

WHAT IS A CORPORATION?

Imagine getting together with a group of people to share some common interests. You can meet with your friends, perhaps for a weekly card game, or with neighbors to discuss local politics, or your high school classmates to reminisce the glory days. Your group might be an assembly of business acquaintances, teammates, factory workers, farmers, veterans, soldiers, hobbyists or fellow believers in a god, a philosophy, a public policy, a political cause. Any sort of group, any type of interests.

Since this is a purely imaginary exercise, there's no need for restraint. You can be a group of 21st century parents organizing a youth soccer league in the United States, biblical-era Egyptians building a monument to Osiris, 14th century French weavers convening to set prices for their textiles, 8th century scholars in Mali planning a library, 16th century Aztec warriors planning to attack the invading Spaniards—or any other group in any time and place of your choosing.

Over time, the group grows as more people are drawn to your cause. Infrequent get-togethers become more formal and more regular meetings. The weekly card game begins to look more like a casino; the workers collective takes on the attributes of a union; your policy group, a political party. Planning a library or monument moves forward to the point of building a library or monument. Resisting the invaders means mustering an army of your own.

People have a wondrous capacity for organizing in order to achieve ends that no one person could undertake on their own. The earliest human history was marked by natural collectives of families or clans, but these were soon augmented by groups that convened for reasons other than simple genetic proximity. The challenge of supporting ever-larger and more complex groupings of individuals is nothing less than the story of human civilization.

Figure 1-1: An early meeting place

As its popularity grows, maintaining your group becomes more and more demanding of people's time and available resources. What had started as a casual, intermittent involvement now demands the full-time attention of numerous people and a level of commitment that continues to expand.

Meetings, at first sparsely attended, are now over-crowded. Space is at a premium. Logistics become more and more complex; even the task of feeding and housing everyone requires a sizable expense and effort. Eventually the group becomes large enough that meetings grow past the point of being merely unwieldy. They become enormously difficult, then almost impossible as no one person has the capacity to accommodate everyone.

Wisely, your collective decides to obtain a space of its own. Your group could rent out available quarters, purchase an existing building or even build a headquarters from the ground up. First and foremost, your group needs money and it turns to its members to secure financing. If the group is religious in nature, the financing mechanism might be called tithing. For an educational group building a school, tuition; for a civic group forming a town, taxes; for a guild or labor union, dues; for a charitable group, donations; for a sporting club, membership fees; for a business, ownership, shares; for construction of a sewer system, municipal bonds. Whatever term is used, the acknowledged leader of the group collects the money until the group has enough to rent, purchase or construct a meeting space.

Quite suddenly, the leader of your group dies. The members are saddened, of course, but life goes on. The group appoints a new leader, meetings resume, and planning for the new headquarters moves ahead. But along comes the spouse or child of the deceased leader and says "That money belonged to my kin. Since I'm the rightful heir, the money is now mine."

"Nonsense," says the new group leader. "That money is for our headquarters. It belongs to us. Our deceased leader was just the caretaker for other people's funds"

But the original leader's relation is not convinced. The money isn't immediately accessible to the group. Maybe it's in the old leader's house, and his spouse refuses to let the group members in. Or perhaps it's in the bank, and the banker is hesitant to make it available until disputes have been settled. The individual members in your group begin to worry about the status of their project. "I want my money back. I contributed it for a headquarters, not to pass along to an heir who isn't even part of our undertaking."

The dispute needs to be settled in some fashion that depends on the mores and structure of the society in which the group exists. The many ways in which communities resolve their differences are also a central part of the story of human history. A group that is part of a warrior culture might settle its monetary dispute through combat. A group in a feudal society would take the dispute to the lord of the manor and seek his decision on the matter. A tribal group might seek guidance from its chieftain or a council of elders.

A group in a nation committed to the rule of law would take the matter to court.

In our imaginary situation, if the group goes to court it may well find itself disappointed in the outcome:

> Group: *We, the Official Organization of Movers and Shakers, hereafter known as OOMS, demand that the OOMS funds being held by the kin of our deceased leader, be returned to us forthwith.*

Magistrate: *The laws of our nation apply to people. The heir has legal standing in the eyes of the law. The individual members of your group each have their own standing as well and they can each petition the court to try and get their money back. But OOMS...your group! It's not a 'thing' the law recognizes. It has no identity to speak of.*

Group: *But the money belongs to OOMS. It's ours!*

Magistrate: *A simple sense of fairness tells me the money should stay within your organization. But the law tells me otherwise. Without any standing, this court cannot rule in favor of your group, as it doesn't really exist...at least as far as the law is concerned.*

It's a conceptual oddity. The group is recognized in one way or another in the minds of its members (and others) as something distinct from the individuals that comprise the group. But no such recognition arises in the courts until the laws of the land explicitly embrace the concept of a group as having a legally-recognized identity of its own.

The organizational concept that OOMS is looking for is the *corporation*. Tribes, clans, and feudal societies don't have much need for corporations. Societies based on the rule of law do. The existence of a formal legal entity for a group of people that is distinct from the individuals comprising the group allows the group a legal presence it could not otherwise have. The group—the *corpus*—can retain its identity and its legal rights as a corporation, even as the members of the group come and go. "We will make your organization an artificial person," the law in effect is saying, "so that you can have standing within our legal system, just as a natural, biological person does. You can enter into contracts. You can be recognized as a legitimate party in lawsuits. You can exercise legal rights."

"You can keep your money."

So right off the bat, we have one obvious advantage of incorporating. An incorporated group, a *corporation*, can be recognized in a court of law as an entity with a legal standing more or less equivalent to a person.

The concept of corporate personhood does not usually sit well with the public at large. Corporations are so obviously *not* people that the idea of legally granting them equal standing with individuals seems patently absurd. But not recognizing a collection of individuals as an entity distinct from the members themselves also leads to absurdities, such as OOMS not being able to retain its funds. Once that obstacle is overcome—once corporations are granted legal status—then the accumulated results of thousands of individual cases involving corporations serve to refine and define just what a corporation is and what its rights and responsibilities are under the law.

Sometimes, the cumulative effect of case law restricts corporate rights. But more frequently, it seems, court decisions and legislative actions add to the legal status that corporations enjoy. As corporations have gained additional rights that previously had belonged only to individuals there has been considerable push-back on the concept of corporate personhood, spurring a modern re-examination of the corporate rights and corporate responsibilities that have accumulated over centuries.

The notion of a corporation as a formally-recognized fictitious person is frequently traced back to the 13th century Catholic Church (though its roots can certainly be extended even further). Pope Innocent IV (1243-1254) issued a rule allowing an ecclesiastical corporation (a *collegium*) to deliver an organizational oath through a single individual because, as the Pope declared, "the College is in corporate matters figured as a person." The organization could be sworn in, in other words, much as an individual could. But corporate personhood had its limits. Only individual people, not corporations, could be excommunicated since the latter is a mere "legal term" and is not capable of sin. Even at this early date, the 'first' corporation gained a lopsided type of personhood, obtaining a convenience available to individuals without taking on the moral onus of possible sin. That imbalance notwithstanding, corporate personhood was intended as a concept of convenience and nothing more.

Thomas Hobbes, writing in Leviathan in 1651, referred to corporations as "…lesser commonwealths in the bowels of a greater, like worms in the entrails of a natural man." Hobbes' point was that the state—the only grouping of people that really mattered to Hobbes—was put at risk by hosting a multitude of smaller groupings—corporations—within its framework. Hobbes viewed the proliferation of corporate entities, of the business variety as well as incorporated towns, churches and other entities, as so many smaller parasites feeding off the host of the nation-state. His objections notwithstanding, Hobbes was a shareholder in the Virginia Company, one of the earliest European corporations.

In the modern world, it no longer seems advisable to think of corporations as "lesser" anythings. The largest business corporations—the multinational giants like Shell Oil, Walmart, Toyota, Apple—operate on a scale of finance and influence that make them secondary to few other entities on the planet. Since business corporations first came into being there have been giants among them—think of the British East India Company, for example. But formal incorporations remained a relatively rare form of doing business until late in the 19th century. With the dawning of the 20th century, corporations became more commonplace—so much so that we easily use the term *corporation* to refer to a business corporation, without feeling a need to distinguish it from other types. As corporations grew in size and number, so did their power.

The First Corporations?

The often-reliable Wikipedia begins its entry for Standard Oil with this paragraph:

> Standard Oil Co. Inc. was an American oil producing, transporting, refining, and marketing company. Established in 1870 by John D. Rockefeller as a corporation in Ohio, it was the largest oil refiner in the world of its time. Its controversial history as one of the world's first and largest multinational corporations ended in 1911, when the United States Supreme Court ruled that Standard Oil was an illegal monopoly.

The paragraph captures a lot:

- the status of Standard Oil as among the "largest" and "first";
- the importance of oil and transportation as key industrial sectors;
- the prominence of the infamous "Robber Barons", John D. Rockefeller among them;
- the tendency of corporations towards monopoly control;
- the emergence of the "multinational" corporation;
- the controversy surrounding almost all large corporations;
- the role of the courts in reigning them in.

Unstated, but perhaps implied in the paragraph, is the leading role of the United States in the emergence of the corporate form of business and in creating conditions in the late 19th and early 20th centuries for corporations to thrive.

Corporations existed before Standard Oil, of course. But not terribly many. A study of corporations in 18th century America tallied a total of 317 business corporations: 62 financial firms, 207 highway and canal companies, 36 utilities, 8 manufacturers and another 5 listed as miscellaneous. The corporate model of doing business in the United States didn't really begin to pick up steam until after the Civil War and even then, involved fairly small-scale enterprises for the most part.

Standard Oil was something new. The world's first multinational corporation, as Wikipedia puts it, or the first modern corporate behemoth, to put it another way. Standard Oil was the exemplar of the corporate "trust", a complex web of business entities that often disguised the role of the oil giant as the one pulling the strings. The trust allowed Standard Oil to exercise enormous influence in the booming business of petroleum through its direct operations as well as through controlling interests in, or outright ownership of, other companies.

Standard Oil's dominance of the industry was great enough that the company produced more petroleum than could effectively be marketed in the United States, compelling Rockefeller to seek markets overseas. In the 1890s, Standard Oil began selling product in China under the *Mei Foo* brand, a phrase that translates to American Trust. Soon thereafter, Standard Oil began marketing operations in the Middle East as well. By the early 1900s, half of Standard Oil sales were outside the U.S.

The company's influence over the petroleum market—and related activities, like rail transport—was enormous. Ida Tarbell, writing in her groundbreaking work, The History of Standard Oil, characterized the company's operations this way:

> There is no gaming table in the world where loaded dice are tolerated, no athletic field where men must not start fair. Yet Mr. Rockefeller has systematically played with loaded dice, and it is doubtful if there has ever been a time since 1872 when he has run a race with a competitor and started fair.

Eventually, the courts of the land would agree with Ms. Tarbell's assessment. Standard Oil exercised too much influence over the petroleum market. This particular trust was busted as an illegal monopoly—disbanded by the 1911 Supreme Court decision, echoing Tarbell's sentiment in the legalistic parlance of the courts:

> The unification of power and control over a commodity such as petroleum and its products by combining in one corporation the stocks of many other corporations aggregating a vast capital gives rise, of itself, to the prima facie presumption of an intent and purpose to dominate the industry connected with, and gain perpetual control of the movement of, that commodity and its products in the channels of interstate commerce…

Put simply, Standard Oil was a giant, multinational corporation. But is it fair to tag it—as Wikipedia does—as the *first* giant, multinational corporation? Long before Standard Oil came into existence—before the United States itself was formed—numerous companies operated on a global scale, their international reach typically reflected in their names: British East India Company; Dutch East Indies Company; Hudson's Bay Company.

One such multinational, *The Governor and Company of the merchants of Great Britain, trading to the South Seas and other parts of America, and for the encouragement of fishing*, better known to history as the South Sea Company, inspired such reckless investing early in the 18th century that Britain was compelled to pass the Bubble Act of 1720 in an attempt to forestall rampant speculation in other companies. The South Sea Company reminds us of modern scandals like Enron or Bernie Madoff's investment company—mostly smoke and mirrors, with no *there* there.

For the most part, these 16th and 17th century multinational firms had charters from their respective governments that brought each firm into legal existence and allowed for its operation. These were corporate charters. The firms were corporations.

An Early Charter

Early charters were quite explicit in the terms laid out for the corporate entities. This was true for the Dutch East Indies Company, but it is its sister corporation, the Dutch West India Company, that has an especially revealing charter, one that is almost breath-taking in its scope. The corporate charter of the Dutch West India Company, signed on June 3, 1621 was written in a manner that is dense and (in a surprisingly recognizable fashion) highly legalistic, but a few excerpts give the flavor of how tightly woven together were companies and countries in the 17th century.

The charter begins civilly enough:

> The States-General of the United Netherlands, to all who shall see these Presents, or hear them read, Greeting.

It then lays out a noble-sounding mission:

> …with mature deliberation of counsel, and for highly necessary causes, found it good, that the navigation, trade, and commerce, in the parts of the West-Indies, and Africa, and other places hereafter described, should not henceforth be carried on any otherwise than by the common united strength of the merchants and inhabitants of these countries; and for that end there shall be erected one General Company, which we out of special regard to their common well-being, and to keep and preserve the inhabitants of those places in good trade and welfare, will maintain and strengthen with our Help, Favour and assistance as far as the present state and condition of this Country will admit: and moreover furnish them with a proper Charter, and with the following Priveleges and Exemptions

and goes on to detail the exclusive authority of the Dutch West India Company:

> ...for the Term of four and twenty Years, none of the Natives or Inhabitants of these countries shall be permitted to sail to or from the said lands, or to traffic on the coast and countries of Africa from the Tropic of Cancer to the Cape of Good Hope, nor in the countries of America, or the West-Indies...nor in the western or southern countries reaching, lying, and between both the meridians, from the Cape of Good Hope, in the East, to the east end of New Guinea, in the West, inclusive, but in the Name of this United Company of these United Netherlands.

In other words, a large portion of the known world, from Africa to the Americas, was being ceded (as far as the Netherlands were concerned) exclusively to the Dutch West India Company for the next twenty four years. Woe to those who ignore the corporation's chartered rights:

> ...whoever shall presume without the consent of this Company, to sail or to traffic in any of the Places within the aforesaid Limits granted to this Company, he shall forfeit the ships and the goods which shall be found for sale upon the aforesaid coasts and lands; the which being actually seized by the aforesaid Company, shall be by them kept for their own Benefit and Behoof. And in case such ships or goods shall be sold either in other countries or havens they may touch at, the owners and partners must be fined for the value of those ships and goods...

The Dutch West India Company could enforce laws, seize property, and levy fines on merchant sailors. The company's authority is not just ocean-going, however:

"...moreover, the aforesaid Company may..."

> *(bullets added for clarity)*
> - make contracts, engagements and alliances with the princes and natives of the countries comprehended
> - build any forts and fortifications there
> - appoint and discharge Governors, people for war, and officers of justice, and other public officers, for the preservation of the places, keeping good order, police and justice, and in like manner for the promoting of trade
> - advance the peopling of those fruitful and unsettled parts

Nor is the corporation thus chartered left to its own devices:

> ...if it should be necessary for the establishment, security and defence of this trade, to take any troops with them, we will, according to the constitution of this country, and the situation of affairs furnish the said Company with such troops, provided they be paid and supported by the Company....Which troops, besides the oath already taken to us and to his excellency, shall swear to obey the commands of the said Company, and to endeavour to promote their interest to the utmost of their ability.

There is much more in the 55-Article, 5,000 word charter, including exemptions from taxes, rules for sharing the spoils of war, details of company management and organization, requirements for meetings and accounting reports, and even instructions for the appropriate company action if a ship is blown off course. But the main thrust of the document is the creation of a business entity to carry out the expansionist aims of the Dutch government through exploration, conquest, settlement, piracy, and commerce. As was typical of the business charters of the 17th, 18th and well into the 19th centuries, the corporations thus created were granted exclusive monopolies to conduct the business at hand. Corporations—far from fostering competition—were one of the key mechanisms by which monarchs constrained the marketplace and stifled competition because such limitations were seen to be in the nation's best interests.

Corporate Traits

So what makes Standard Oil the first multinational?

A history of the corporation, written in 1917, starts out with a caveat: *"The term 'business corporation' has no precise technical significance."* That's still the case today; the idea of the "business corporation" means different things in different contexts. This is not to say the term is meaningless. But there's enough variability in its use to make it difficult (perhaps impossible) to say, for instance, whether the first true multinational business corporation came into being in 19th century America or 17th century Europe.

An ordinary dictionary definition of 'corporation' seems fairly straightforward. It's generally worded along the lines of: *a corporation is a group of individuals acting as a single entity, and recognized as such under the law.* The definition allows for the wide variety of corporate entities in existence. A corporation comes into being when the collection of individual people goes through the legal process of incorporating as defined in the jurisdiction in which they have filed their corporation documents. The definition is typically silent about the size of the collection. A corporation can be twenty people, or twenty thousand, but no matter the number, the end result is a single, legally-recognized entity. *E pluribis unum*...Out of many, one.

In more common use, though, 'corporation' generally refers not only to a business entity, but to a sizable business operation. In this context, the term takes on some additional detail. Business textbooks typically list five traits of a business corporation, the first being its just-mentioned status as a legal entity. The four additional traits are:

Limited liability: As a legal entity, a corporation is entitled to enter into binding contracts, borrow money, and do other things that business people do. The corporation bears the responsibility for fulfilling these contracts, but individual corporate shareholders do not. They are shielded from most of the financial liability that the corporation assumes. For an unincorporated sole proprietorship, there is no distinction between the business and the business owner—if the business is successfully sued, the owner is fully liable so that even his personal finances and property are at risk. A shareholder in a corporation, on the other hand, is off limits in a lawsuit. His or her potential losses are limited to the value of the shares owned.

Transferable shares: Corporations are divided into shares, each share conferring a small bit of ownership in the corporation. Shares of a corporation are alienable, that is, readily transferable from one person to another. Corporate shareholders can transfer their shares in fairly unrestricted fashion. In some business arrangements, this is not the case. A shareholder in a partnership, for example, may not be permitted to dispose of her shares until the company is dissolved.

Perpetual existence: Corporations are immortal...or at least, they have the potential to be. Since the corporate entity is a "fictional person", its existence is not limited by the finite lifespans of natural persons. Even if the entire board of directors and senior managers of a corporation were to perish in some disaster, the corporate entity still survives. Of course, the potential for perpetual existence is no guarantee of achieving it. Very few corporations manage to survive century after century.

Centralized management: Shareholders of a corporation are, collectively, the owners of the company. But typically, management of a corporation is handed over to a group that is distinct from the bulk of the shareholder community. A board of directors, appointed by the shareholders, sets the strategies and policies for the corporation while the day to day operations are managed by senior corporate executives.

Standard Oil clearly possessed at least three of these five traits. It was a discrete, legally-recognized entity that filed its articles of incorporation in Ohio on January 10, 1870. Limited liability of business corporations was a fairly well-established legal principle in the United States by the late 19th century, so Standard Oil can be said to possess that corporate trait as well. The company's "immortality" was available in principle, even though Standard Oil was ultimately dismantled by the Supreme Court.

Other corporate traits are murkier. Shares in the company were originally held by 37 shareholders, and were eventually combined into a trust that conveyed the shares to John D. Rockefeller and eight other trustees. It's an open question as to how “alienable” these shares were in practice, though there does not seem to have been any actual legal or contractual prohibition on their transferability. So too with separation of management and ownership that is characteristic of modern corporations; shares of

Standard Oil were held by such a small cadre that it's hard to conceive of any shareholders that did not have an active part in the running of the company. (On the other hand, the actual corporate web of Standard Oil's ownership of and holdings in other companies was quite complex, making it difficult to say just how many actual shareholders the company had, or who was running what).

How does Standard Oil stack up against its 17th and 18th-century corporate cousins in Europe? A description from Palgrave's Dictionary of Economics of one such firm, chartered in 1602, provides a useful comparison:

> The Dutch East Indies Company...was formed as a limited time venture. When that limit drew near, the board boldly announced that the corporation would persist indefinitely. The shareholders sued to force a liquidating dividend—and lost! Fortunately, they found they could sell their shares to other investors for the value of a liquidating dividend—or even more. Thus was born the first modern stock market, and the alienability, or unhindered sale, of shares became a defining characteristic of a corporation. Letting shareholders realize their investments by selling their shares, rather than liquidating the business, gave corporations a second defining characteristic: indefinitely long lives...

By one count, then, it's possible to construe the Dutch East Indies Company (not to be confused with the Dutch West India Company, which came a few decades later) as "more" of a corporation than Standard Oil. It was a legal entity chartered by the Dutch government. Shares in the company, originally untransferable, became alienable through the board's actions; the company even established the Amsterdam Stock Exchange, considered the first such corporate shares market in the world. Similarly, the limited 21-year existence envisioned by the original charter was expanded to an indefinite existence, and the firm remained a viable venture for almost 200 years. The description above implies a corporate management separate from the firm's ownership. The status of limited liability is uncertain and, as far as we know, was not tested by the legal system of the time. Thus, the Dutch East Indies possessed four of the five traits in the above list, one more (perhaps) than our count for Standard Oil.

But checking off the corporate traits is probably missing the point. Neither firm really "feels" like a modern corporation. The Dutch East Indies Company, with its aggressive posture of exploration and colonization is more of an invading force on behalf of the Dutch government than an independent business venture. The company essentially waged war, occupied territory, and exercised government-like powers such as coining money, running prisons and carrying out executions. We can reasonably suppose that most readers would agree that Standard Oil, with its focus on domestic petroleum production, is much closer in spirit to a 21st century corporation than the exploratory mission of its 17th century predecessor, but even here, the restricted ownership rights and massive, monopolistic presence distinguish Standard Oil from its modern corporate brethren.

The Dutch East Indies Company and Standard Oil are both corporations, but they are conceptually and operationally quite different from one another and both are quite different from a modern corporation. Most large corporations that do business in the marketplace of modern capitalism have a set of common traits that are not fully captured by the conventional list we laid out above. They do indeed possess the five listed traits—legal entity, limited liability, alienability, potential immortality, and central management—but these alone are not enough to distinguish corporations of centuries past from those of the modern age.

The conventional traits are necessary but not sufficient—necessary for organizations to be described as corporations, but not sufficient to make for a full description. We have identified several additional traits that also belong to corporations. They are useful in distinguishing the modern-day corporation from its historical predecessors.

Non-monopolistic: Corporations from centuries past, such as the Dutch West India Company, operated as monopolies, with sole control of goods being traded and trade routes over which they moved.

In the modern era, corporations are actively discouraged from becoming dominant enough in the marketplace to act as a monopoly. Companies that do reach such size and influence risk being dismantled by government fiat—as happened to Standard Oil in 1911 and AT&T in 1982. There are certainly exceptions to this, such as incorporated utilities or corporations in emerging economies that may be more tolerant of (or even encourage) monopoly status. Aramco, the Saudi Arabian petroleum giant, is certainly a monopolistic corporation within Saudi Arabia even as it competes against other oil companies on the world market. As a general rule, though, modern corporations do not operate as monopolies.

Non-restrictive charter: Corporate charters in the 17th and 18th centuries (and well into the 19th) granted companies significant rights but also imposed substantial restrictions on a company's operations. Charters could be lengthy, legalistic and highly detailed. The 1621 charter for the Dutch West India Company was more than 5,000 words divided into 55 discrete articles that defined what the corporation could and could not do. Activities that extended beyond the charter were legally deemed to be *ultra vires* (beyond the powers) and thereby illegitimate.

The practice of governments of awarding a small number of specifically defined corporate charters eventually gave way to the modern practice of the bureaucratic rubberstamp: fill out some forms, pay a fee, identify an agent and *voila*…you are now a corporation. Modern corporate charters are brief and do not define or restrict the business activities of a company in any meaningful way.

Public reporting: Most, but not all, modern-day business corporations are subject to substantial financial reporting requirements. These reports are available not only to shareholders of the company, but to the public at large, a requirement intended to promote transparency of business operations. This is certainly true for publicly-held companies (those traded on the stock markets). But private firms are also subject to reporting requirements, especially large financial corporations holding investor or customer assets. Even small corporations are subject to some straightforward reporting requirements as they must file a publicly-available list of corporate officers and agents.

Expansive Personhood: For as long as corporations have existed as a legal concept, they have been endowed with legal 'personhood'. However, corporations in the modern era have achieved a considerably more expansive set of rights associated with corporate personhood, as a result of numerous policy decisions and court actions. The 2010 U.S. Supreme Court decision, Citizens United v FEC, held that the federal government had no authority to restrict spending by corporations that were exercising their Constitutionally-protected right of free speech, even in the context of 'hot button' political issues. Citizens United is a non-profit corporation, but the decision extended to business corporations as well.

Although this expanded concept of corporate personhood is perhaps most notable in the United States, it seems to be operable throughout most of the corporate world in the sense that corporate persons are able to speak (and spend) just as freely—or with similar restrictions—as the biological citizens of the country in which the corporation operates.

One central characteristic of the business corporation that is not included in the list of either conventional or expanded traits is the goal of making money. The aim of turning a profit lies at the heart of business ventures, whether corporate or otherwise, so much so that including it as a specific trait seems superfluous. In corporate parlance, the drive to make money is sometimes expressed as a responsibility to "maximize shareholder value." The idea was expressed in perhaps its purest and most aggressive form in the 1970s by the economist, Milton Freidman. No one can argue with the idea that corporations exist to make money; Freidman took the notion to its extremes. As laid out in his famous article, *The Social Responsibility of Business is to Increase its Profits*, any activity by corporate executives that did not increase profitability—philanthropy, for example—made them the "unwitting puppets of the intellectual forces that have been undermining the basis of a free society these past decades." We will return to the question of social responsibilities later in this book.

Public firms—companies like Facebook that are traded on the world's stock markets, as opposed to privately incorporated firms like the candy company Mars, Inc.—are the companies most readily recognizable as 'corporations' when either the conventional set or the full set of corporate traits are taken into consideration.

This is because corporations grow more corporate-like as they grow larger and as they make a transition from private to public ventures. Traits like transferability of shares and separation of management from ownership are clearly attached to large, public companies but less clearly to privately-held firms. A private firm may have only a few dozen shareholders while large public corporations can have more than a million shareholders owning company stock.

In common parlance, then, corporations are the big boys, the companies that find their way onto the Fortune 500 list or those that are traded on the major stock exchanges in New York, Tokyo, London or other financial capitals. Of the six million or so business corporations in existence in the United States, only about 10,000 are listed as publicly traded companies on the major stock exchanges. With these large, public companies so dominant in the business world, it's hardly surprising to find the meaning of 'corporation' gravitating in that direction.

This is not an absolute! Private companies count, as do the millions of smaller business corporations that dot the economic landscape around the world. There are also several types of specialty corporations such as, in the U.S., so-called "S" corporations which extend the legal protections of a corporation to businesses that are, essentially, partnerships with a limited numbers of shareholders. These corporations do not adhere as closely to the textbook definition as do larger firms.

Corporations and Size

The largest multinational corporations are often compared to nations in terms of their economic presence and enormous breadth of their activities. At one time, corporate land holdings could be nation-sized in scale. The British East India Company occupied most of India for the better part of a century. The Dutch East India Company ruled large tracts of Indonesia for almost two centuries. The Hudson's Bay Company held an area known as Rupert's Land that was one-third of present-day Canada including most of Manitoba and Saskatchewan along with sizable chunks of Alberta, Ontario and Quebec. Even as recently as the 1980's, Coca-Cola purchased 14% of the land area of Belize in order to grow oranges, only to scuttle its plans due to environmental and social backlash.

In the 21st century, corporate presence and scale tends to be felt more in financial terms than in land holdings. Wal-Mart, with a half a trillion dollars in annual revenue is the "same size" as Norway, with half a trillion in GDP. Royal Dutch Shell, perhaps ironically, operates on the same financial scale as Iran. BP roughly equals South Africa.

Fortune's Global 500 list for 2019—its list of the world's largest corporations—had combined revenues of $32.7 trillion, about $13 trillion larger than the GDP of the United States. The combined GDP's for all nations, or the Gross World Product, was $86 trillion. Five hundred corporations account for more than a third of the global economy! Roughly one out of every three dollars spent in the world flows through the coffers of these industrial giants. One of every three tons of ore, gravel, or sand pulled out of the ground, one out of every three trees felled for timber, one out every three tunas, or lobsters, or haddock fished from the seas, one out every three ears of corn or bales of cotton, one out of every three shirts, or dolls or spools of wire is being dug, cut, seined, grown, woven, assembled or extruded for this small group of 500 companies.

One could argue the legitimacy of the company-to-country comparison. GDP attempts to measure "value added", a different and less straightforward measure than corporate sales. Economists differ as to the best metric for comparing corporations and countries. Attempting a more apples-to-apples comparison, one study compared corporate and country revenues, and found that, of the 100 largest economies, 29 were countries and 71 corporations. Perhaps a truer number for the Global 500 is one out of every five, or one out of every ten, rather than one out of three dollars or tons or goods coming under their collective umbrella.

But debate on economic accounting would miss the main point. There is no arguing the overwhelming dominance of these few companies in the global economy, or the impact they have on the movement of materials out of the earth, into the market-place, then back to the earth again as wastes. And there is no arguing the scale of the impact these companies have on the lives of human beings. It is not just dollars and materials flowing through the corporate machinery. About 70 million people work directly for the Global 500, and hundreds of millions of others work for suppliers to them and distributors for them.

Walmart has more workers (2.3 million) than the U.S. military has soldiers (2.1 million, active and reserve), more customers in a week (260 million) than Indonesia has people (258 million) and stores enough to completely cover the island of Manhattan…twice. Coca Cola sells over 690 billion drinks per year, roughly 100 drinks per person for every man, woman and child on the planet; about three percent of what people around the world drink is a Coca Cola product. McDonald's used to proudly report the number of hamburgers it sold but stopped updating its figures in 1994 when the total reached 100 billion. More than two billion people—one-fourth of the world's population—use Facebook as a form of social communication.

The credit reporting company, Equifax, "…organizes, assimilates and analyzes data on more than 800 million consumers and more than 88 million businesses worldwide," according to the company's website. Equifax is a modest-sized company, far too small to make the Fortune 500 list, yet a breach of its data base put at risk the personal credit information of hundreds of millions of people.

Royalties and taxes from Royal Dutch Shell's operations in Nigeria contribute substantially to that nation's overall economy; petroleum accounts for 75 percent of the government's national budget, and Shell produces about half the country's oil. A Shell power plant produces 14% of Nigeria's electricity. Shell is large enough to be a visible slice of the global energy pie…it accounts for two percent of the world's fossil fuel production and, not surprisingly, accounts for two percent of greenhouse gas emissions around the globe when emissions from company operations are combined with emissions from the combustion of Shell products.

Luxembourg-based ArcelorMittal, the world's largest steel company, produces six percent of the world's steel. Vale S.A. in Brazil mines 15% of the world's iron ore. De Beers sells more than one third of all the uncut diamonds in the world. Toyota and Volkswagen, the largest car makers on the planet, manufacture more than 20% of the world's vehicles. Saudi Arabia is funded almost entirely by the revenues from the national oil company, Aramco. It is reputedly the world's largest corporation, worth about $2 trillion, about twice the size of Apple, the largest US company.

An organizational entity through which hundreds of billions of dollars flow, be it a firm or a nation, is an entity that wields enormous influence: over millions of jobs; over technological development; over the creation of new wealth; over the use of media; over invention; over cultural norms; over exploration and expansion into new realms. Entities this large can create massive disruptions: large scale unemployment; poisoning of the environment; abuse of workers; devastation of communities; wholesale deception; destruction of whole ecosystems; cultural impoverishment; financial disruption; cooption of political processes. When Occupy Wall Street or Bernie Sanders rails against "corporate greed", they are not referring to the incorporated village of Lynbrook, NY, or the Tuckahoe Recreation Club Inc. in Virginia. They're talking about giant, multinational firms—companies that take actions impacting millions of jobs, billions of lives and trillions of dollars.

The impact of large business is not all negative, of course. We admire corporations for their innovation, their familiarity, their ability to nourish us, entertain us, enrich us, thrill us, to build the future, and as Elon Musk or Richard Branson like to remind us, to just be so cool sometimes. They are risk-takers, innovators and—as the history of corporations reminds us—explorers of new frontiers.

CHAPTER 2

THE AGE OF DISCOVERY AND THE EMERGENCE OF CORPORATIONS

When Christopher Columbus sailed the ocean blue, he did so not only with the blessings of Queen Isabella and King Ferdinand of Spain, but with their solid financial support. The Spanish monarchy, eager to outpace rival Portugal in empire building, funded Columbus' 1492 voyage in hopes the explorer could fulfill his promise of finding a new sea route to Asia. Columbus' agreement with the monarchs was formalized in the Capitulations of Santa Fe, a brief document that was more or less a contract. The Capitulations detailed the obligations and responsibilities of both parties, including granting the explorer a life-long title of Admiral and promising him ten percent of whatever riches were generated from his journey (a promise that led to centuries of litigation for Columbus and several generations of his heirs).

Although the Capitulations offer no details on the actual financing of Columbus' journey, Isabella and Ferdinand generously provided the explorer his three caravels—innovative sailing ships that had proven themselves under open-ocean conditions—and funds for provisioning the ships and paying his crew. Their generosity had its limits, though. Rather than shell out cash, the monarchs punished the port of Palos for violating its fishing restrictions by requiring the city to provide ships to Columbus.

A few years after Columbus' revelation of a new world across the Atlantic, another Italian explorer, Giovanni Caboto, took on the Anglicized name of John Cabot and approached King Henry VII of England for sponsorship of another voyage across the Atlantic. Cabot became the first European (other than the Vikings) to reach the shores of what would eventually come to be called North America. The king obliged in 1497, granting Cabot and his sons a brief charter giving the explorers the right "to find, discover and investigate…" as yet unknown lands. But the English king's generosity stopped there. The charter granted to Cabot and his crew made

Figure 2-1: The ships of Columbus by Gustav Closs, 1892

and his crew made perfectly clear that the journey was to be "…at their own proper costs and charges." Henry's 1504 sponsorship of Cabot's son, Sebastian, for another journey to North America was similarly frugal, leaving the funding for the exploration entirely to explorers.

The different financial arrangements are not hard to fathom. Spain was ascendant, flush with its victory over the Moors and on its way to piecing together one of the largest empires the world has ever known. It could be expansive with its funding for explorations as well. England, in the early 16th century, was more of a backwater. The country had only recent emerged from the tumultuous decades of the War of the Roses There was no British Empire to speak of. National finances were insecure—creation of the Bank of England was still a century away. England had some empire-building ambitions, perhaps, but a much smaller capability than Spain to dip into the royal coffers and fully fund an exploratory fleet.

Both the Spanish and English monarchies hoped that their sponsored explorations would lead to future riches for their respective realms; Spain had the wherewithal to fund the expedition up front in the speculative hopes of seeing substantial returns; England did not share the same appetite for risk. But even the Spanish Empire's largess had its limits. When Ponce de Leon set sail for Florida in 1513, he was flying the flag of Spain, but the trip was funded without any financial support from the Crown.

The 1500's in Europe were the golden era of global discovery, with names straight out of grade-school history texts. Along with Christopher Columbus and Ponce de Leon, Spain sponsored Ferdinand Magellan and Hernando de Soto. England sent forth John and Sebastian Cabot, along with Francis Drake, Walter Raleigh, Henry Hudson, John Smith, and others. Amerigo Vespucci, for whom the Americas are named, sailed for Portugal, as did Vasco da Gama. Giovanni de Verrazano was sponsored by France.

Each exploration required ships, instruments, maps, provisions, a crew, weapons, insurance policies, port fees...and a means to pay for it all. Financing was sometimes provided by monarchs, sometimes by individual explorers who were wealthy enough to self-finance, sometimes through loans from wealthy individuals or a nascent banking system, sometimes from the pooled resources of partners and, often, through a combination of these sources. Spain, flush with wealth from its silver and gold trade, eventually organized the Spanish Treasure Fleet later in the 16th century. Under the leadership of Pedro Menéndez de Aviles (who founded the oldest European settlement still in existence in St. Augustine, Florida), the fleet relied on royal sponsorship and financing to carry out its mission of shipping explorers, settlers and supplies to the New World and returning with precious metals, gems, spices, lumber and whatever other riches could be extracted.

With increasing frequency, however explorers without access to the largess of wealthy monarchs were turning to a new source of funding: the corporation. Modern corporations were invented as a convenient way of combining funds from a potentially sizable pool of investors. As explorations became lengthier and increasingly adventurous, they became both more expensive and considerably more risky. Think of an exploration as a highly speculative 16th-century business start-up. There is a chance for investors to see spectacular profits but it would be years before they are realized; after The Virginia Company settled Jamestown, the company did not see a profit for more than a decade. The corporate form of financing offered advantages that a traditional partnership could not. The nature of those advantages holds the key to the historical emergence of the business corporation.

The Merchant Adventurers

Corporations of one sort or another were in existence long before the 16th century. Towns, counties, universities, churches, hospitals, trade guilds and numerous other entities were formal corporations. The city of York in England was incorporated by royal charter in 1396. Historians of commerce trace business corporations back at least as far the Roman Empire, whose *publicani* were a sort of early government contractor/tax collector with some recognizable features of a modern corporation. Grain mills in 14th century France had distinctive features of corporations, including pooling of funds, sharing of risk and issuance of shares.

Corporations as a model and means of doing business on a global scale had to wait until 16th century England to take on a recognizable form with the formation of the *Mystery and Company of Merchant Adventurers for the Discovery of Regions, Dominions, Islands, and Places unknown,* more casually known as the Merchant Adventurers (an 'adventurer', as the word was used at the time, was a merchant involved in a business venture. It seems to have as much the meaning of venture capital as it does 'adventure' in the modern sense). The Merchant Adventurers was founded by Richard Chancellor, Sir Hugh Willoughby and the aged and venerable explorer, Sebastian Cabot, who was appointed Governor of the company. Cabot was the son of John Cabot, who sailed to North America in 1497, just five years after Columbus' historic voyage. Along with the three founders, the Company had about 240 shareholders who invested 25 pounds each to fund its activities. The company convened in 1551, received a charter from King Edward VI in 1552, and launched its first expedition in 1553.

As the company's exceedingly long name implies, the scope of operations of the Merchant Adventurers included the entire globe, or at least the reaches of it not yet discovered by previous explorers. Their first expedition was eventful. Willoughby, an English military hero with no naval or nautical experience, commanded the small fleet, but was separated from the other ships by bad weather and stranded in the cold north, where he and his crew eventually perished off the coast of Norway under somewhat mysterious circumstances. Despite being trapped in ice, the ship was well-provisioned with enough food and fuel to enable survival. Some historians have suggested that the crew succumbed to carbon monoxide poisoning.

Richard Chancellor had more success, making port in a remote part of Russia. Chancellor travelled 600 miles inland, largely by horse-drawn sleigh, to arrive in Moscow and parlay with Ivan the Terrible, a first step in establishing more formal trade relationships between the two countries. Chancellor made a second voyage to Russia in 1555, returning to the England the following year with a passenger from Moscow, Osip Nepeya, the first Russian ambassador to England. Close to home, however, Chancellor's ship capsized in a storm off the coast of Scotland and Chancellor perished. Nepeya survived and eventually made his way to London.

The Merchant Adventures looked to build on their initial successes without having to reinvent themselves from scratch—a step towards corporate perpetuality. The company was formally re-chartered by Queen Mary I in 1555, and then again by Queen Elizabeth in 1566. A name change was in order, reflecting the company's focus on Russia, and given, as Elizabeth noted, that the original name "…is long, and consisteth of very many words…" Documents at the time refer to the group by several different names but they eventually became known as the Muscovy Company (or the Russia Company….take your pick).

The re-chartering and open-ended continuation of the group was a key step in the corporatization of the Muscovy Company. It not only gained legal recognition as a corporate entity, it also gained the capacity for perpetual existence characteristic of modern corporations. The company's charter called for it to be regarded as "…thenceforth one body, and perpetual fellowship…both in deed and in name." The open-ended nature of the charter was a significant shift from the general practice of the time (and of later times as well) of issuing charters that specifically limited the lifespan of the chartered company.

In other words, the group of several hundred shareholders were now granted a corporate identity and a perpetual existence, and could not only conduct its business, but own property, collect rents, file legal suits, and be sued. Though not stated in so many words, the Muscovy Company had achieved legal personhood.

The charter also specified a corporate-style management arrangement for the company. The shareholders had no involvement in running the company—another key feature of modern, publicly-traded business corporations. Their only explicit role was in annually electing a governing board. The board, on the other hand, had no substantial limits on its authority, other than to adhere to several stipulations of the charter, such as a requirement to use English ships and crew.

The company also innovated its finances. The Muscovy Company raised funds that were not earmarked for a specific venture. As the Encyclopedia Britannica notes, the firm "…was the first English joint-stock company in which the capital remained regularly in use instead of being repaid after every voyage." Thus, it was not only the company's legal existence but its managerial board and finances that enjoyed the prospects of (potentially) perpetual existence. The company also foreshadowed the practices 19th-century "trusts" by becoming substantial owners of other corporations. When the Turkey Company was chartered by in 1580, 9 of the 12 individual shareholders in the Turkey Company were also key investors in the Muscovy Company, and the Muscovy Company itself—as a corporation—had substantial holdings in the Turkey Company.

The loss of two company principals at sea—Willoughby and Chancellor were dead within three years of the Muscovy Company's first voyage—emphasizes the value of the corporate form. Had Columbus died, it's not at all clear that his repeated missions to the New World would have continued. But the deaths of two key founders of the Muscovy Company did not slow the company's efforts. Its status as a legal entity independent of the individuals that comprised it provided corporate continuity. A formally-comprised board of directors facilitated ongoing operations. The company's innovative financing allowed it to continue exploring and trading. The mechanism of securing a modest amount of funds from each investor, and multiplying investments across a large group of investors was critical to the long-term operation of the firm.

The Muscovy Company held a monopoly on English-Russian trade for the next century and a half. For a while, it was something of a corporate superstar. The Lord Mayor of London was a shareholder, as were other distinguished citizens, including Henry Hudson, whose grandson of the same name would sail on several expeditions for the Muscovy Company (before meeting his death at the hands of a mutinous crew). Queen Elizabeth found the company an indispensable instrument of not only foreign trade, but foreign affairs, appointing Muscovy Company dignitaries as Ambassadors to Russia and instructing them to, among other things, arrange a marriage between the Czar's daughter and English nobility (the effort failed).

Though entitled to perpetual existence, it met the fate of most corporations in that the firm was eventually dissolved. The firm's fortunes changed after its first century of business, losing out to other trading companies. It's efforts to maintain a monopoly met with pushback as anti-monopolist sentiment took its toll. The Tsar grew to resent England's insistence on barring trade from other countries and in 1571, rescinded many of the rights that had been granted to the company. Still, the Muscovy Company survived as a business until the Russian Revolution in 1917, a corporate lifespan of more than 350 years.

The Muscovy Company has a credible claim as the world's first business corporation. From the time of its founding there was no turning back. There were fits and starts and periods of long inactivity on the corporate front, but the arc of history is clear: The global rise of corporations had begun.

CHAPTER 3

FROM UNCOMMON TO COMMONPLACE

The rise of corporations did not proceed smoothly nor was it particularly rapid. The Muscovy Company was followed by a number of other global trading corporations whose names are well-known to history: the Dutch East Indies Company, the Dutch West India Company, the Hudson's Bay Company, and the founders of Jamestown, the Virginia Company. The largest of them all, the British East India Company, was a giant with unparalleled influence, accounting for (if Wikipedia is to be believed) half of the world's trade in the company's heyday. But for several centuries, the corporate form remained very much the exception to the rule, with only a handful of companies successfully beseeching a monarch or a legislature for the right to incorporate.

The corporate charters issued by England, Holland, other European countries typically granted companies nothing less than an almost complete monopoly with authority that modern firms can only dream of. Even companies with fairly modest charters—a monopoly on exporting wool, say—were legally empowered to restrict others from doing business, levy fines against those who traded without permission, and confiscate illicitly marketed goods. The corporations that embarked on grand explorations could board vessels, seize ships, and impress seamen. They sometimes operated as extensions of a country's military power, and could build forts, raise armies in defense of their monopolistic merchant rights, and govern vast swathes of territory. These powers served the chartered companies well and benefited the monarchies that received a substantial portion of the income generated by the firms, often building empires in the process.

Not everyone was pleased with the corporate way of doing business. Monopolies, after all, have a way of raising hackles, as was the case with Muscovy Company's lost rights in Russia. Not quite fifty years after the Muscovy Company received its initial charter, Queen Elizabeth appeared

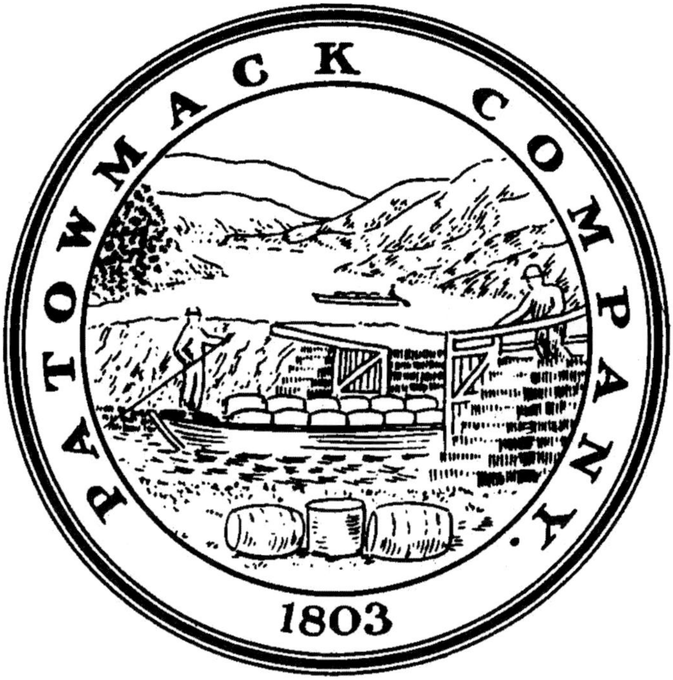

Figure 3-1: George Washington's Potowmack Company was the first corporation with its roots in America

before Parliament in 1601 and gave what has come to be known as the Golden Speech. It was also, in many respects, Elizabeth's farewell speech, as the queen died the following year. In large measure, the Golden Speech was the Queen's response to a groundswell of anti-monopoly sentiment that had arisen in Parliament. Elizabeth had used monopoly grants as a key fund-raising tool (necessitated, she felt, by Parliament's frequent reluctance to fully fund the Queen's requests), but the monopolists were widely viewed as taking unfair advantage of their privileges, angering both the common people and nobles alike. The Golden Speech included Elizabeth's admission of widespread abuse of monopolistic grants, an explanation of how such abuses came about, and a promise to remedy the problems at hand. It is considered a masterstroke, as it successfully, albeit temporarily, diffused a tense political situation.

> Of my self I must say this, I never was any greedy scraping grasper, nor a strict fast-holding Prince, nor yet a waster; My heart was never set upon any worldly goods, but only for my Subjects good…And if my princely bounty have been abused, and my Grants turned to the hurt of my people contrary to my will and meaning, or if any in Authority under Me have neglected, or converted what I have committed unto them, I hope God will not lay their culps to my charge .

As if to cement the matter, the Elizabethan courts, in the year after the Golden Speech, decided a landmark case, Darcy vs. Allein, in which the Queen's grant to Edward Darcy of monopoly rights over the production and sale of playing cards was ruled an illegal monopoly. The case stands as an important milestone—both in clarifying the status of monopolies and as an assertion of the authority of the courts in the face of regal privilege—and has come to be known as the Case of Monopolies.

Monopolies and corporations were not synonymous, of course. Edward Darcy's charter granting a monopoly on playing cards pretty much applied to a one person and included few of the characteristics of a corporation. But with the creation of the Muscovy Company, the corporate form was emergent. Over time, anti-monopoly sentiment and anti-corporate sentiment became practically indistinguishable.

Leap ahead to the time of Adam Smith and the beginnings of industrialized capitalism, as we understand it today, and the corporate form begins to receive some critical analysis. In the Wealth of Nations, Smith used the term 'corporation' about fifty times. But the meaning is not always recognizable to our current sensibilities. Smith is critical of corporations for, among other things, keeping wages unnaturally high; hardly a complaint one would expect to hear in modern times. Corporations were a barrier to Smith's notion of efficient capitalism. They interfered with the effective functioning of the market, from Smith's point of view, by reducing (or eliminating) competition rather than being part of an economic system that fostered it. In his chapter on market prices, Smith writes of corporations:

> ...They are a sort of enlarged monopolies, and may frequently, for ages together, and in whole classes of employments, keep up the market price of particular commodities above the natural price, and maintain both the wages of the labour and the profits of the stock employed about them somewhat above their natural rate.

There are certainly those in the 21st century who would agree with some aspects of Smith's 18th century characterization, especially regarding corporations qua monopolies. But Smith wasn't referring to corporations as we know them today. The Wealth of Nations largely focuses on merchant corporations—what we would call guilds—and their ability to carve out local monopolies that restricted competition, limited trade, controlled access, and dictated both the wages of tradesmen and the price of the goods they made. These were the weavers, wheelwrights, hatters, coachmakers, pin makers, and innumerable other tradespeople that dominated manufacturing prior to the emergence—just getting underway in Smith's day—of large-scale factories that came to characterize the industrial revolution.

Smith had a bit more tolerance for trading companies, offering a begrudging acceptance that some monopolistic authority is helpful in starting up an enterprise focused on exploration and trade—but only temporarily. Overextending monopoly rights led to what Smith termed "the Absurdity and hurtfulness of almost all our chartered companies" adding "Negligence and profusion must always prevail…in the management of such a company".

Smith had more to say on the topic, bemoaning the tendency of the corporations to produce poor-quality goods:

> ...The pretence that corporations are necessary for the better government of the trade, is without any foundation. The real and effectual discipline which is exercised over a workman, is not that of his corporation, but that of his customers. It is the fear of losing their employment which restrains his frauds and corrects his negligence. An exclusive corporation necessarily weakens the force of this discipline. A particular set of workmen must then be employed, let them behave well or ill. It is upon this account that, in many large incorporated towns, no tolerable workmen are to be found, even in some of the most necessary trades. If you would have your work tolerably executed, it must be done in the suburbs, where the workmen, having no exclusive privilege, have nothing but their character to depend upon, and you must then smuggle it into the town as well as you can...

A corporation, as Smith uses the term, is a form of monopoly. The two terms are almost equivalent in Smith’s day, despite the anti-monopoly sentiments that entered English political discourse at least as far back as Queen Elizabeth’s reign. The guilds in Adam Smith’s England typically operated on a fairly small and local scale.

For the few large enterprises that existed, such as the East India Company, Smith had a bit more tolerance, recognizing the advantages of creating a temporary monopoly enterprise:

> ...When a company of merchants undertake, at their own risk and expense, to establish a new trade with some remote and barbarous nation, it may not be unreasonable to incorporate them into a joint-stock company, and to grant them, in case of their success, a monopoly of the trade for a certain number of years. It is the easiest and most natural way in which the state can recompense them for hazarding a dangerous and expensive experiment, of which the public is afterwards to reap the benefit....

Even here, Smith's enthusiasm for the corporate form was more apparent than real:

> ...These companies, though they may, perhaps, have been useful for the first introduction of some branches of commerce, by making, at their own expense, an experiment which the state might not think it prudent to make, have in the long-run proved, universally, either burdensome or useless, and have either mismanaged or confined the trade....

By the time of The Wealth of Nation's third edition, Smith was even more convinced of "the Absurdity and hurtfulness of almost all our chartered companies." And he added a new critique of the joint-stock model of corporate ownership: "Negligence and profusion must always prevail, more or less, in the management of such a company," he concluded.

The term 'corporation' hadn't yet gelled in the 18th century to take on its current meaning. Smith was writing at the cusp of the intersection between the age of mercantilism and the industrial revolution. Corporations—far from being the hallmark of Smithian capitalism—served as obstacles to the practice and spirit of the type of capitalism Smith was describing. Competition—a concept at the very heart of Smith's work—was absent, or at least severely constrained, in the monopolistic corporate settings of the 18th century.

The Corporation and the U.S. Constitution

Whether through mistrust of the corporate form, bureaucratic reluctance to issue new corporate charters, or the presence of alternative and viable forms of business, sizable corporations remained a rarity from the time of the Muscovy Company through to the 19th century. Legally, the concept of a corporation was well-enshrined. Blackstone's Commentaries, published in the 1760s, included a substantial write-up in a chapter, On Corporations (which, revealingly, was included in the section On the Rights of Persons). Blackstone formally describes the situation we rather informally postulated in our opening Introduction: the dilemma of an unincorporated group trying to resolve legal questions of rights and property:

> To show the advantages of these incorporations, let us consider the case of a college in either of our universities, founded ad studendum et orandum [for study and prayer], for the encouragement and support of religion and learning. If this was a mere voluntary assembly, the individuals which compose it might indeed read, pray, study, and perform scholastic exercises together, so long as they could agree to do so: but they could neither frame, nor receive, any laws or rules of their conduct; none at least, which would have any binding force, for want of a coercive power to create a sufficient obligation. Neither could they be capable so retaining any privileges or immunities: for, if such privileges be attacked, which of all this unconnected assembly has the right, or ability, to defend them? And when they are dispersed by death or otherwise, how shall they transfer these advantages to another set of students, equally unconnected as themselves?
>
> …with regard to holding estates of other property, if land be granted for the purposes of religion or learning to twenty individuals not incorporated, there is no legal way of continuing the property to any other persons for the same purposes, but by endless conveyances from one to the other, as often as the hands are changed. But, when they are consolidated and united into a corporation, they and their successors are then considered as one person in law: as one person, they have one will, which is collected from the sense of the majority of the individuals: this one will may establish rules and orders for the regulation of the whole, which are a sort of municipal laws of this little republic; or rules and statutes may be prescribed to it at its creation, which are then in the place of natural laws: the privileges and immunities, the estates and possessions, of the corporation, when once vested in them, will be for ever vested, without any new conveyance to new successions; for all the individual members that have existed from the foundation to the present time, or that shall ever hereafter exist, are but one person in law, a person that never dies: in like manner as the river Thames is still the same river, though the parts which compose it are changing every instant…

Colleges, towns and all sorts of other entities could incorporate, but in Blackstone's time, few large businesses took advantage of this specialized legal status. As the 1700's drew to a close, no country in Europe had even close to 1,000 corporations, a statement that remained true well into the 1800's. In the newly formed United States, corporations were even less numerous. There were scarcely ten U.S. corporations in 1790, about 100 in 1795 and still fewer than a thousand in 1800, though at that point, fairly rapid growth had put the U.S. roughly on par with England, France and Germany (Prussia) in terms of the number of incorporated businesses.

The 19th century saw a sea change in the United States. Corporate formations went from a trickle to a roaring flood, so that the growth of corporations in the U.S. soon far outpaced the rate of growth in Europe. From less than 1,000 corporations in 1800, America's pool of business corporations grew to 10,000 in the 1840s and 20,000 in the 1850s. By 1860, the U.S. had approximately 26,000 incorporated businesses, compared to about 7,000 incorporations in Britain, another 7,000 or so in France and a much smaller pool in Germany.

America had considerably more total "authorized capital" (the amount permitted to be raised per the terms of the corporate charter) in its corporate universe than did any country in Europe. U.S. data after 1860 is spotty, but by 1916, when America first introduced a corporate income tax, 341,253 corporations filed tax returns, a more than thirteen-fold increase over the 1860 data. In the early years of the 20th century, about 60% of the world's business corporations were U.S. companies.

(Note, however, that the data on corporations are not easily comparable, either between years or between countries. Different numbers can reflect different types of business formations. Early records were often cumulative without taking into consideration businesses that have folded whereas later data sometimes present counts of only existing businesses. However, the numbers provide a reasonable broad brush comparison of incorporation activity between years and between countries).

The rapid rise of corporations in the United States is due in part to the unusual status of corporations in the Constitution. This remarkable document—one that anticipated so many critical federal issues that would shape the nation—was entirely silent on the matter of incorporation.

Not that the founders were lacking opinions on the subject. A general sentiment antagonistic to corporations was certainly in the air in pre-Revolutionary America. The Boston Tea Party, after all, was as much in opposition to the British East India Company—the empire-building corporate powerhouse that was already almost two centuries old—as it was to the British government. The company was accused in one widely-circulated pamphlet of "tyranny, plunder, oppression and bloodshed." At the same time, however, the desire to build a self-reliant economy in the United States led some to see the desirability of empowering the federal government with the authority to create corporations.

James Madison was perhaps the chief proponent at the Constitutional Convention in favor of a federal incorporation authority, introducing language—innocuous to a modern ear—that Congress "…shall have the power to grant charters of corporations in cases where the public good may require them and the authority of a single State may be incompetent." Benjamin Franklin, ever practical, found Madison's language overly broad and recommended the authority be limited to corporations for "cutting canals". George Mason, fearful of abusive monopolies, opposed Madison's broad language but was able to live with Franklin's more limited suggestion.

But even a sharply-narrowed focus on canals was too much for some delegates. The language succumbed to what one Constitutional scholar labeled the "strong prejudice in the Convention and afterwards... against...authorizing Congress to charter corporations". The solution to the conflicting opinions on corporations was to simply leave the Constitution silent on the topic. Indeed, there is very little actual material in the records of the Congressional Convention dealing with the matter. Jefferson briefly noted that chartering authority was rejected "...except that of giving copyrights to authors and patents to inventors, the general power of incorporating being whittled down to this shred."

In a later debate in 1791, regarding incorporating a national bank, Alexander Hamilton firmly took the opposite view:

> A strange fallacy seems to have crept into the manner of thinking & reasoning upon the subject. Imagination appears to have been unusually busy concerning it. An incorporation seems to have been regarded as some great, independent, substantive thing-as a political end of peculiar magnitude & moment; whereas it is truly to be considered as a quality, capacity, or mean to an end. Thus a mercantile company is formed with a certain capital for the purpose of carrying on a particular branch of business. Here the business to be prosecuted is the end; the association in order to form the requisite capital is the primary mean. Suppose that an incorporation were added to this; it would only be to add a new quality to that association; to give it an artificial capacity by which it would be enabled to prosecute the business with more safety & convenience.

With only a small handful of corporations in existence at the time, the topic may have struck the delegates as more a matter of principle than of functional necessity. As history unfolded, Congress did in fact decide to authorize an occasional federal corporation. But in very large measure, corporate charters were left to the individual states. This apparently minor decision turned out to have enormous consequences for the direction the nation's economy was to take.

The United States, by unconscious design, became a nation without a national mechanism for chartering new businesses. Instead, the country was a collection of thirteen individual former colonies, each a sort of mini-nation, with its own chief executive, legislature, taxes, laws, currencies, customs and chartering authority. This was a sharp divergence from the situation in Europe, where the fledgling United States drew most of its legal precedence and culture. Monarchs in Europe chartered corporations in a process that, more and more, was being relegated to administrative bureaucracies acting on the monarch's behalf. No such federal entity existed in the U.S. This omission separated the United States from its European heritage as distinctly as any other feature of the new nation.

Businesses ended up receiving articles of incorporation from individual state legislatures. At the outset, these were still companies with a very different look and feel from a modern corporation. They were largely what can be thought of as a "mixed enterprise"—a private company formed to execute a specific public goal, and receiving its mission, support, authority, direction, timetables, restrictions and, sometimes, financing, from the chartering state. These were not the empire-building corporations of an earlier era but were instead focused on turning states that were still mostly wilderness into the units of a functioning country, with the roads, bridges, waterways and services needed for a modern nineteenth century nation.

A quick history of one such firm will give a feel for the earliest of these unambiguously American corporations.

The Potowmack Company

In September of 1784, just a year after the end of the Revolutionary War and five years before he became president, George Washington left the comfort of his Virginia estate for an extended trip to the western territories of the United States. The purpose of his journey, in part, was "...to obtain information of the nearest and best communication between the Eastern and Western Waters; and to facilitate...the Inland Navigation of the Potomack."

Washington felt the Potomac River to be the most promising means of commercial transportation between the developing businesses in the eastern states and the vast territories that lay to the west and stretched out towards the Mississippi River. Such commerce was essential not only for economic growth, but for political purposes as well. Washington wanted to cement the allegiance of the territories to the United States in the face of considerable economic, political and cultural influence from the Spanish, French and British in these areas. America's expansive destiny in these early years was anything but manifest.

The largely coastal populations of the original thirteen colonies were well-served by ocean-going vessels that could handily move goods from port to port. But as the nation expanded westward, the need for inland transportation routes became more pressing. Agricultural goods and raw materials needed to move west to east to meet the demands of populated areas and people and supplies needed convenient routes into the west as the area was settled.

Water transportation struck Washington as much more practical than trying to develop land transportation routes through the roadless, mountainous and untamed wilderness of Appalachia. But a water route would not come easily. The Potomac, as with other potential river routes to the west, was not fully navigable. Segments of the river needed to be dredged, canals needed to be built, and portage roads were necessary in order to make a viable transportation route linking the Potomac to the Ohio River and other western waters. Washington hoped to form a corporation to do the work and turned to his friend, James Madison, for help in obtaining the necessary charters.

Since the Potomac River forms the boundary between Maryland and Virginia, both states would have to agree to the work to be done to improve its navigability. Beyond that, Washington and Madison hoped that the states themselves would actively support the project through a grant of both authority and direct financial assistance. Madison (who would soon become the key proponent for adding corporate charter authority to the Constitution) met with legislators and governors, drafted and redrafted legislative proposals and by 1785 achieved his goals. The Maryland and Virginia state legislatures approved nearly identical language to bring the Potowmack Company into existence through a formal charter. The creation of the company is a significant and underappreciated milestone in the economic history of America. It was not only the country's first corporation without ties to England, it was also America's first attempt at a major infrastructure project. And it was the first time anywhere that a multi-jurisdictional corporation was brought into existence, as remarked by the American Historical Association:

> The creation of the Potowmack Company by the concurrent action of different states marked a distinct advance in the progress of political science. Never before in the history of the world had two distinct sovereignties united in such a step. Here were the same individuals sustaining similar political relations to different governments, constituted in each an artificial person, dealing under one name with property in each, and amenable in each to the supervision of its authorities.

It's unlikely that Washington, Madison or any others involved in the creation of the Potowmack Company saw it in such grandiose terms. Madison simply pursued a pragmatic solution to the quandary created by operating a single corporation in a multiplicity of jurisdictions: seek authority from each.

The two state legislatures did more than simply create a new company and leave it to its own devices. The charters, and subsequent legislative actions, specified its mission and timetable, granted government-like authorities, proscribed corporate governance, stipulated engineering requirements, created a financing mechanism and provided direct financial support. The details are worth fleshing out as a means of clarifying the nature of early American corporations and the differences to their modern-day counterparts.

The charters "for opening and extending the navigation of the Potowmack river" effectively issued 500 shares of the Potowmack Company, valued at 50,000 pounds sterling. Virginia and Maryland each subscribed to 50 shares, and Virginia agreed to another 50 shares that were to be turned over to George Washington in honor of his war service to the country. Washington was embarrassed by the gift, and eventually wrote the shares into a trust for a college. He did accept an offer to serve—unpaid—as the company's first chief executive. In total, the two states subscribed to 30% of the company's shares, with the remainder available to the public.

The fact that purchasers "subscribed" to shares warrants some explanation as the subscription process was very different from modern sales of corporate stock, and the differences turned out to be quite problematic for the fledgling corporation. Shares were purchased at only a small fraction of their face value; the purchase entailed a commitment of future payments to the company towards the total value on a more or less as-needed basis. The legislative provisions called for share payments to be made only in specie—gold or silver coin—prohibiting the use of paper money.

The charters, as were typical of the era, spelled out the work of the Potowmack Company in some detail. The company was required to complete initial improvements to river navigation in three years and to build canals and locks within ten years. A number of engineering specifications were included, such as the requirement that the river remain navigable to flatboats drawing a foot of water or less, even during dry season. In return, the company was granted explicit authorities, such as the exclusive right to collect tolls on the river, and the ability to condemn lands on the river bank when needed for company works (essentially, eminent domain). Such requirements and authorities were commonly used in English company charters to bring about desirable river improvement projects; they now found their way into the Potomac River project.

Initial enthusiasm for the project ran high and even in the cash-poor (and in particular, coin-poor) new country, the Potowmack Company managed to secure commitments on 400 of its 500 shares even before its first shareholder meeting. The “pledge now, pay later” subscription process minimized much of the risk for shareholders. If the company was successful, investors would be holding valuable shares at little upfront cost. If the company failed, the prospect of the board of directors successfully collecting on its subscriptions was distant.

Washington hired James Rumsey in 1785 to supervise the operations of the new company. Washington had met Rumsey a year earlier when he stayed at Rumsey’s inn in Bath, Virginia (present day Berkeley Springs, West Virginia). Rumsey had impressed Washington with his engineering know-how and his innovative concepts in boat design for river navigation, a topic we’ll revisit in Chapter 6, on patents. The future president doubtless hoped Rumsey could bring the same ingenuity to the formidable challenge of preparing the Potomac River for navigation. Rumsey spent a year at the task before resigning in frustration, his resignation readily accepted by the equally frustrated company directors.

The full trials and tribulations of the Potowmack Company are beyond the scope of this book, but the project turned out to be overly-ambitious from an engineering, managerial and financial perspective. The Potomac River did not yield easily to the efforts to channelize its depths and bypass its more energetic falls. Animals, equipment and labor were all in short supply. Ironworks were a rarity and at considerable distance from the worksite, so that any heavy equipment needs resulted in long delays and large expenses.

The workforce was particularly problematic. In the sparsely-populated region, lacking in infrastructure needed to support a sizable crew, managers for the Potowmack Company had to, in essence, scrounge the riff-raff for workers, hiring prisoners, ex-prisoners and aimless veterans of the Revolutionary War. Fights, thievery and scuffles with the local populations were constant problems. Rumsey's workforce was so disorderly and troublesome that, he complained to Washington, "officers of justice durst not go on the grounds to execute their offices" from fear of being manhandled by ruffian workers.

As for finances, the going was bleak, as one historian noted:

> As work began, the company issued frequent subscription assessments, but the pay-as-you-go subscription process and the requirement that pledges be paid in specie quickly confronted the realities of the Maryland-Virginia agricultural economy in the 1780s. Drought and insect invasions plagued the area in 1785 and were followed by torrential rains in 1786, which ruined crops and the regional economy. Such natural disasters were made worse by a general American malaise fostered by large war debts and the surplus of commercial credit. As a result, by the end of 1786 less than half of the assessment had been met. Even the state of Maryland, with tax revenues dwindling, felt the squeeze and defaulted on payments on its fifty shares.

The Potowmack Company was not without some initial successes, as it did manage to construct canals allowing passage around the Great Falls of the Potomac River. But the company's financial and managerial situation slowly and steadily worsened. Defaults on existing shares increased. Attempts at raising money by selling new shares were unsuccessful, as were odd efforts at fundraising through a sort of shareholder lottery. Legal entanglements became the norm—the company had a protracted six-year dispute with Virginia governor Henry "Light-Horse Harry" Lee (father of Robert E. Lee) over property along the river, and it's unclear if the matter was ever settled. Although the company managed to survive, on paper, until 1828, it accomplished very little after its first decade of operations and, beyond its success at Great Falls, had not much to show for its overall existence of more than 40 years.

Corporations and the General Charter: The War Between the States

In the absence of federal incorporation authority, the task of chartering corporations in the United States fell to the legislatures of the thirteen original colonies, but the number of decision-making bodies grew as the nation expanded. At the start of the Civil War, 34 American states were called upon to decide not only where their allegiances lay, but which businesses within their borders were significant enough to become a corporation.

Each new incorporation required an act of a state legislature to create a corporate charter (or, occasionally, a coordinated effort among multiple legislatures, as was the case with the Potowmack Company). Each charter required a negotiation to determine terms—the corporate mission; the monopolistic privileges available to the corporation; the fees it could charge others; its rights to lands and natural resources, the financial contribution of the state, and, just as importantly, the explicit limitations and obligations written into the charter: the number of years the corporation could exist; the monies due from the corporation to the state; corporate responsibilities for public utilities; the cap on corporate financing that was included in most charters.

The legislators themselves had a mix of experience and concerns. Mistrust of the English-style trading companies ran strong and the belief that monopolies posed a fundamental, ongoing threat to democracy itself seemed written into the early American character. Charters, by granting exceptional privileges to a select group were even seen as contrary to the principle of "natural rights" that so gripped the founders of the new country. "All charters granting exclusive rights are a monopoly on the great charter of mankind," one early legislator opined, explaining that it's not the well-being of corporations that is paramount: "The happiness of the people is the first law."

But the perception grew that incorporation was, on occasion at least, a useful tool for financing the numerous large projects and large institutions required to support the needs of the young nation. The class of men who became legislators overlapped considerably with the class of men who started and grew businesses, lending a certain self-interest to sporadic acts of incorporation. The mixed emotions surrounding corporations were reflected in state laws. For example, New York's constitution of 1821 (the state's second) explicitly permitted the creation of corporations but set a high hurdle, requiring the approval of two-thirds of both houses of the legislature in order to bring one into being.

New York's approach was not unusual. As one historian described it:

> …the American system…put the emphasis on restrictions and accountability measures, rather than on privileges. State constitutions and statutes reinforced the restrictive stance towards corporations...charters tended to be granted sparingly, in keeping with the widespread belief that the potential for corporations to accumulate power rendered them inherently dangerous to democracy.

But anti-corporate sentiment gradually gave way to a practical need to foster new businesses, and negotiations over corporate charters became more frequent. The horse-trading involved was often fevered and complex. When Aaron Burr wished to charter a bank in New York in 1799, opposition from the handful of other functioning banks in the state was fierce. The state legislature ultimately agreed to charter a new venture, but not without dumping some large and costly tasks on the new venture. But the corporation gained some unprecedented flexibility as well.

Burr's business emerged as a strange hybrid, with a key responsibility for supplying drinking water to New York City. Burr had chartered a waterworks instead of a bank! The language in the charter was unusually—one could say exceptionally—broad and it's not clear that any of the legislators, other than Burr himself, truly recognized its significance:

> It shall and may be lawful for the said company, to employ all such surplus capital as may belong or accrue to the said company in the purchase of public or other stock, or in any other monied transactions or operations, not inconsistent with the constitution and laws of this State or the United-States, for the sole benefit of the said company.

In other words, the company could do what it wanted with its surplus funds, a degree of freedom almost unheard of at the time. Burr, as one observer put it, "…realized that he could smash the barrier distinguishing a waterworks from a bank with a sentence." The charter was easily approved (Burr, himself a state legislator, presumably voted in favor). His new enterprise would spend some of its capital to upgrade the water supply to the city of New York, as per its obligations, and was free to use the remainder of its finances—which turned out to be the great bulk of its funding—for other businesses as the company saw fit. Burr saw fit to establish a bank, The Manhattan Company, which is the predecessor of today's JP Morgan Chase bank.

Charters for other businesses in New York and elsewhere were not, at first, as permissive as Burr's charter, but were equally varied. When City Bank (yes…that Citibank) and Bank of America were chartered by New York, both in 1812, each was required to pay a substantial sum in support of the New York City school system. Some charters granted limited liability to shareholders, others withheld it, some adopted "double liability" or "proportional liability", and still others granted limits to liability only under certain conditions. Many charters—along with the underlying state laws regarding corporations—were simply silent on the matter of personal shareholder liabilities for corporate activities.

Businesses were expected to support a wide variety of projects for the public good, regardless of any connection to the nature of the business itself: support to schools, universities, asylums, hospitals and orphanages; funding of infrastructure like roads, canals, gaslights and even hotels; requirements to support other businesses by buying and holding their stock. Banks were instructed by their charter as to what interest they could charge and the proportion of loans to go to farmers or manufacturers. River works, like those of the Potowmack Company, had their tolls and fees set by charter.

The incorporation of a company to build a bridge between Cincinnati, Ohio and Covington, Kentucky (today known as the John A. Roebling Suspension Bridge) brought forth some of the more unusual charter language of 19th century America. The bridge, oddly enough, was largely constructed during the Civil War, even though it connected Yankee Ohio with Confederate Kentucky. Planning for the bridge had begun prior to the war and somehow proceeded even after hostilities broke out. In addition to stipulating much of the bridge's engineering and finances—location, height requirements, distribution of shares, corporate management structure, and toll rates—the Kentucky charter for the Covington and Cincinnati Bridge Company included language acknowledging the great issue of the day dividing North and South:

> …it shall be unlawful for said company, their agents or officers, to suffer any slave or slaves to pass over said bridge without a written request of the owner or owners of such slave or slaves, or without said slave or slaves shall do so in the company of such owner or owners. And said company shall be liable to pay to said owner or owners for every slave or slaves so permitted to pass contrary to the provisions of this act, the full value of said slave or slaves, to be ascertained by the verdict of a jury, together with a penalty of ten per cent ..

From Kentucky's perspective, at least, an important charter stipulation for protecting the public good!

Not all charter stipulations targeted the public good. Charters not only granted a privilege for one company to do business, but frequently restricted others from engaging in competitive businesses, harking back to the monopolistic grants of the English trading companies. Corporate governance was assigned by charter, some opting for one-share-one vote, others for one-shareholder-one-vote, and others, still, with a hybrid approach to shareholder voting. Would-be companies often engaged in intense lobbying—to gain favorable provisions, prevent unfavorable charter language, or forestall competitors from receiving charters of their own. Lobbying easily led to bribery, and graft was considered rampant, at least as far as some historians of business are concerned:

If the early U.S. corporate system had so many features that might seem to require corporations to be more responsible to society in comparison with our current system, we might reasonably ask why it was gradually abandoned. The answer is that chartering corporations by special acts of state legislatures was a system susceptible to corruption. Incumbent corporations would bribe or otherwise induce legislators and legislatures to prevent new corporations from entering and competing with them. And corporate wannabes would use the same techniques to gain charters.

The anti-charter, anti-graft sentiment coalesced around the Populist sentiment, "Equal rights for all. Special privileges for none," a slogan that helped propel Andrew Jackson to the Presidency in 1828. Once in office, President Jackson vetoed the rechartering of the Second National Bank in 1832—a rare example of a federally-chartered corporation—referring to such charters as a "…prostitution of our Government to the advancement of the few at the expense of the many…" (One of the Bank's strongest defenders in Congress was Senator Daniel Webster, who was kept on retainer by the bank for his legal services).

Graft and privilege were key factors working against continuation of the special charter system, but state legislatures also found themselves increasingly burdened by chartering requests. The growth of the nascent American economy, combined with emerging technologies (most notably, the steam engine), and a maturing financial system spurred not only an increase in the number of new businesses, but an increase in business size. As operations moved from small, home-based manufactories and services to larger factories, banks, insurers, and utilities, the need for corporate-style financing and the demand for incorporation services grew precipitously. This was particularly true in the northern states, where those with capital and ambition had fewer opportunities than in southern states for investing in large-scale agricultural endeavors and so looked to manufacturing and finance for investment opportunities.

The absence of a national chartering system also influenced the dynamics of the day. States found themselves in competition with other states for the right to charter new businesses. When Maine cleaved from Massachusetts in 1820 to become its own state, it adopted its own set of laws. Unlike Massachusetts, with a chartering statute that imposed unlimited liability on corporate shareholders, Maine's chartering authority provided for limited liability, a much more attractive option for would-be corporate investors. Massachusetts found itself in direct competition for investor dollars with Maine and other states that—from an investor point of view—provided limited liability and other attractive terms in their chartering authorities.

The manufacturing community in Massachusetts took note, publishing an 1830 pamphlet, "Reasons for Repealing the Laws of Massachusetts, Which Render the Members of Manufacturing Companies Personally Liable for Their Debts." The authors noted Maine's considerable advantage:

> One of the first public acts of our sister state of Maine, after its separation, was to repeal these destructive laws...of personal liability in manufacturing corporations

The pamphleteers decried the flight of capital from Massachusetts, and a state of affairs they found unjust, embarrassing, injurious, financially ruinous, inconsistent, unintelligible and even harmful to widows and orphans:

> ...Because, if a man die actually with a million of dollars, owning the small sum of one thousand dollars, in several such corporations, his whole

> estate may be taken for the debts of such corporations, and his wife and children reduced to want and misery.

United by language and a common currency, and unhindered by national borders, people and capital could move much more readily between states in the U.S. than they could between countries in Europe. Government policies that were overly oppressive, ineffective or predatory regarding corporations were much more likely to take hold in entrenched European monarchies than under the American system of multiple—hence competitive—incorporating authorities. Corporations could essentially charter-shop in the U.S. for the environment deemed to be friendliest towards a new business. In time, the elimination of constraints on having actual operations in a state of incorporation would make this flexibility even more pronounced.

The nineteenth century in America saw an almost complete transition away from chartering by "special acts" and the adoption, in one state after another, of the general charter—a relatively simple registration process to bring a new corporation into existence with the filing of required forms, payment of a fee and no restrictions at all specific to the new business other than the rules applying to a the necessity of obeying the laws applying to all corporations in the state. Limited liability, which had been an infrequent and sporadic feature of corporate law, became the order of the day as more and more states sought to catch-up to the corporate-friendly sort of legislation adopted by Maine.

This transition to the general charter, brought about by new laws and court cases, provided the framework that built the modern corporation and transformed the United States into (as Robert Wright put it) the world's first "corporation nation". The transition can be divided into three periods that almost divide the nineteenth century into thirds:

1800-1840: The period of incorporation by special charter. A few states begin to adopt general charter authority, but it is not put to widespread use.

1840-1870: A hybrid period, where corporations were formed by both special charter and through the bureaucratic authority of general charters.

1870 onwards: General charters become the rule, as special charter activity is abandoned and, in many states, explicitly and even constitutionally prohibited.

As the transition from special to general charter mechanisms took place, the very nature of corporations changed, coming more and more, in law and practice, to resemble their modern form. The restrictions that special charters imposed began to drop away. Initially, the easing occurred in particular sectors like banks or railroads, as states sought to encourage activities in these areas, but the changes were eventually applied across the board to the entire business community. The limits on the length of time a company could do business were lessened or done away with altogether, minimizing or eliminating the need for frequent (and often costly) charter renewal. Gone, too, were most of the limits on the amount of capital a corporation could raise or the types of business activities it could engage in.

The entire character of corporate charters changed. Whereas special charters were designed to spell out the specific public goods that a corporation was to provide, in exchange for the privileges of incorporation, the general charter treated corporations themselves as a sufficiently beneficial public good, so that no further stipulations were needed. The United States was rapidly emerging as a world industrial power. Corporations were a driver of economic growth, a provider of employment, a creator of societal wealth and a lynchpin of national expansion. They were no longer required to do anything more than attempt to succeed in business. As general charter authorities became the norm, the routine, specific public-interest requirements, such as funding schools, building orphanages, or dredging canals, were completely eliminated.

The reverse was true as well: general charters did not, as a rule, extend special privileges to an individual corporation. Monopoly authority was granted less and less frequently, so that companies wishing to establish banking services, operate a ferry, manufacture tools, drill for oil or engage in the hundreds or thousands of other businesses blossoming in the country had to actively compete with other companies providing the very same service or product. Limited liability became the incorporation norm rather than a specialized endowment. Legislatures grew far less willing to subsidize or actively partner with business ventures, especially after a series of costly bankruptcies in various government-private ventures. Disappearing, too, were the legislative favors that selectively chartered one company while inhibiting its competitors.

Returning to Ohio, home to Standard Oil and (one end, at least) of the Covington and Cincinnati Bridge, we can see these trends at work. As did many states in the mid-19th century, Ohio law explicitly prohibited the use of special charters. Public antipathy toward the perceived graft and cronyism of the special charter system had grown intense, and was directed not only at corporations, but at the entire business of special dealings that were increasingly seen as an abuse of legislative authority. As noted in The History of Ohio Law:

> State subsidization of private companies that produced no public benefits and ran up huge public debts angered many delegates, who insisted that government "leave railroad, canal, turnpike and other corporate associations, to get along upon their own credit, without any connexion or partnership with the State whatever...the whole system may be dug up by the roots, and no single sprout ever permitted to shoot up again"

Ohioans clamored to rewrite the state constitution to eliminate the perceived abuses. The revised state constitution of 1851 included Article XIII on Corporations that began with these two sections:

> Sec. 1: The General Assembly shall pass no special act conferring corporate powers.
>
> Sec. 2: Corporations may be formed under general laws…

By the time the Standard Oil Company was incorporated in Cleveland, Ohio on January 10, 1870, the transition to general chartering authorities was largely complete, although vestiges of the era of restrictive charters still remained. The company's charter is brief, has the ring of boilerplate language, and spells out just a few details of the company:

- The company, named The Standard Oil Company, is being formed under the authority of Ohio's general charter statue passed in 1852
- The purpose of the company is the manufacture and sale of petroleum products
- The capital stock of the company is $1 million, and each share has a value of $100
- The company is chartered in Cleveland, Ohio

The charter is signed by the company owners (both John D. and William Rockefeller among them) and attested to by county Judge Frederick Brand, who essentially acts as a notary public.

It's a reasonable assumption that the Rockefellers and their colleagues had a much easier time incorporating under general authority than would have been the case had they needed to secure a special charter from the state legislature. Still, governments being what they are, the process could be something of a bureaucratic morass. A detailed description of the "cumbersome and time-consuming" process in Delaware in 1875 gives a bit of the flavor of what businesses had to go through:

- Draft a certificate of incorporation signed by at least three people; two-thirds of the signers must be citizens of Delaware
- Publish a newspaper notice of intended incorporation at least 30 days prior to submission
- Submit the certificate to a judge in Superior Court in the county where the company will have its principle place of business. The certificate could only be submitted during periods when the court is not in session.
- The county then publishes a second newspaper notice announcing the application at least three weeks prior to acting on the application.
- If no objections arise to the incorporation, at the next session of the court, the judge submits the paperwork to the Secretary of State.
- The Secretary sends a certified copy to the county Recorder's office, at which point, the company is incorporated.

And you thought your driver's license renewal was cumbersome?

Still, many of the historical restrictions on corporations had disappeared by the latter part of the 19th century. As the Delaware process makes clear, though, states still imposed not just filing requirements, but requirements on how the business could come into being, particularly, residency rules that required both corporate founders and business operations to originate primarily within the state. Some states insisted the corporation have not just a headquarters office but active industrial operations in the state. Even these restrictions would soon vanish.

Delaware in 1875 was not yet the preferred state for incorporation that it is today. That distinction, for a period that straddled the late 19th and early 20th centuries, belonged to New Jersey. The state was ideally positioned between America's two largest cities at the time, New York and Philadelphia, and could readily service the financial and corporate activity in both. Beyond that, New Jersey developed a reputation—one which it worked diligently to secure—as a state friendly to corporations.

Almost all major corporations of the era incorporated in New Jersey, and a substantial portion of smaller company incorporations took place there as well, regardless of where companies were actually headquartered or where they conducted the bulk of their business transactions. New Jersey's rise to prominence as the preferred state for incorporation grew out of a deliberate effort to make itself as corporation-friendly as its legal system and public sentiment would allow. In doing so, it demolished the last vestiges of a system of incorporation based on special charters with restrictive provisions and opened the path to the (more or less) no-questions-asked style of incorporation that dominates today's world of business in the U.S. and in much of the rest of the industrialized world.

Ted Nace, in his excellent (and somewhat ominously titled) book, Gangs of America, begins an exploration of the history of corporations in the United States by citing his own experience as an entrepreneur after his accountant suggested incorporating:

> What's involved?" I asked. "What does it give us?
>
> You go to a lawyer. He'll give you some paperwork, register you with the state, and charge you a couple thousand. In theory it gives you a bit of protection from lawsuits, and it means that if the company goes bankrupt you won't lose your personal assets. The company now will be owned by its shareholders, and your family will have more security because the company is now immortal. If you get run over by a bus, it will go on without you.
>
> That's it?
>
> Yeah, that's it? Pretty much.
>
> Fair enough, I thought, adding "call lawyer re incorp" to my to-do list. A week later, I made the call…

Nace doesn't say where his company incorporated, but the process is similar in all states in the U.S. and in much of the industrialized world as well, all following the simplified incorporating process pioneered by New Jersey.

In need of new sources of state revenue, New Jersey looked to the fees associated with incorporation—both one-time filing fees and recurring franchise taxes paid every year. The state embarked on a deliberate effort over the course of several decades to liberalize its incorporation laws and procedures in order to attract new corporations to the state—regardless of whether they actually conducted business in New Jersey or not. The state had prohibited special charters through a constitutional amendment in 1875, ushering in a straightforward administrative system to register new corporations. Two laws passed in 1888 permitted companies in some sectors to hold stock in other New Jersey companies; in essence, encouraging corporate mergers and unambiguously allowing holding companies and trusts.

Subsequent laws through 1893 expanded this right to almost all sectors and permitted New Jersey corporations to own stock in companies in other states ("foreign corporations") as well as in New Jersey ("domestic corporations"). The laws also granted explicit permission for state corporations to do business in other states, thereby eliminating the geographic restrictions that had been routinely included in charters in decades past. A general corporation law passed in 1896 consolidated most of these earlier changes and removed any last restrictions on the types of business a company could engage in. Each New Jersey corporation was empowered to "create and define" the company's activities.

The liberalization strategy bore fruit. Even New Jersey's fee structure for corporations was simpler and more predictable than the convoluted fee systems in use in other states. Companies began flocking to New Jersey to take advantage of the liberalized rules. Income from chartering fees and franchise taxes quickly rose from an insignificant level in the early 1880s to more than half the receipts for the state by 1900, a remarkably rapid restructuring of New Jersey's finances.

The state budget routinely ran a surplus. "No such showing can be made by any other State," Governor George Werts boasted in 1896, "nor, I apprehend, by any civilized nation anywhere." By 1902, New Jersey had eliminated state property taxes as a no-longer-needed source of revenue. So successful was New Jersey's strategy, which came to be known as chartermongering, that numerous other states—Maryland, Maine, New York, West Virginia and Arizona among them—entered the fray with a similar commitment to liberalization. Delaware, in 1899, adopted New Jersey's corporate legislation practically verbatim. Not content with word of mouth, states began advertising in out-of-state newspapers to entice new incorporations.

New Jersey's success in attracting corporations, and particularly in fostering complex arrangements whereby one corporation could hold a controlling interest in dozens of other companies, ultimately led to the state's undoing as the preeminent destination for corporate charters. New Jersey was the home of America's largest *trusts*—businesses that came to dominate entire sectors of the economy, either regionally or nationally. Of the 318 "industrial trusts" tracked by John Moody around 1900, about half were chartered in New Jersey, as were all seven of the "greater industrial trusts"—the behemoths that completely dominated specific sectors. These near-monopolies in oil, steel and other metals, sugar, and tobacco were—depending on who you asked—the great engines of the American economy or the worst exploiters of the workingman and the American consumer.

Public sentiment turned sharply against the giant trusts, seen as ruthlessly crushing competition, exploiting workers and using their monopoly advantage to overcharge for their goods and services. Ida Tarbell's groundbreaking work, *The History of the Standard Oil Company*, was published in serialized form between 1902 and 1904, and painted a portrait of John D. Rockefeller as "…crabbed, miserly, money-grabbing, and viciously effective at monopolizing the oil trade…". As "trust busting" became a political rallying cry, the appetite on the part of New Jersey's political class for continued chartermongering began to sour. Theodore Roosevelt, who became President in 1901, launched more than forty lawsuits against giant trusts, through the federal Bureau of Corporations in the newly-established Department of Commerce and Labor.

New Jersey also responded to the anti-trust sentiments of the day. Woodrow Wilson, campaigning for governor of New Jersey, ran on a progressive, anti-corporate platform. This was no tangential political issue. It occupied center stage in his campaign. His 1911 inaugural address as governor largely focused on the need to regulate the previously-unfettered activities of the business community:

> If I may speak very plainly, we are much too free with grants of charters to corporations in New Jersey. A corporation exists, not of natural right, but only by license of law, and the law...is responsible for what it creates. It can never rightly authorize any kind of fraud or imposition. It cannot righteously allow the setting up of a business which has no sound basis, or

> which follows methods which in any way outrage justice or fair dealing or the principles of honest industry.

Wilson then urges the legislators to:

> ...effect such changes in the law of the State as will...prevent the abuse of the privilege of incorporation which has in recent years brought so much discredit upon our State.... [S]uch scrutiny and regulation ought not to be confined to corporations seeking charters [but] extended to corporations already operating under the license and authority of the State.

Wilson, as Governor, eventually passed a series of laws that effectively dismantled New Jersey's aggressively favorable incorporating mechanisms. In doing so, he also dismantled New Jersey's major source of state funding and handed Delaware what was to become a clear-cut victory in the race for leadership as the nation's preferred state for incorporations.

The Gospel of Wealth

While distrust of corporations crested in the Progressive Era, not all Americans opposed the rise of corporate power. Andrew Carnegie, one of the first and most visible representatives of America's rapidly growing industrial might, was—among his other legacies—a prolific author. In an 1889 essay with a proud, almost haughty title, The Gospel of Wealth, he wrote:

> The contrast between the palace of the millionaire and the cottage of the laborer with us today measures the change which has come with civilization. This change…is not to be deplored, but welcomed as highly beneficial.

This was one view of the way the country was taking shape. Corporations were successfully amassing capital, employing millions of laborers, creating and then harnessing new technologies. In the process, corporations were revolutionizing life in the United States and throughout the world with new products, new wealth and even new freedoms, as fewer and fewer people were tied to the agricultural way of life that had dominated human history until now. And if a few select individuals became phenomenally, ostentatiously wealthy in the process, those same people were wont to remind us that the wealth is being spread around, so that the great masses of people have so much more than ever before. Carnegie noted that "...the home of the laboring man of our day boasts luxuries which even in the palaces of monarchs as recent as Queen Elizabeth were unknown."

Theodore Roosevelt and Woodrow Wilson likely would have agreed with Carnegie's sentiments…but with caveats. Both politicians were careful to give robust acknowledgment of the many benefits of corporations, seeing them in much the same light as Carnegie, as driving America to a position of increasing wealth and global prominence. But they recognized, as well, the perilous side of concentrating so much economic and political power in the "corporate idea" that Carnegie epitomized. Roosevelt, like Carnegie, celebrated America's industrial might. But throughout his political career, he also feared industrial excess. He wrote, in 1910:

> The greatest evils in our industrial system to-day are those which rise from the abuses of aggregated wealth; and our great problem is to overcome these evils and cut out these abuses…We can not tolerate anything approaching a monopoly…except on terms of such thoroughgoing governmental control as will absolutely safe guard every right of the public. Moreover, one of the most sinister manifestations of great corporate wealth during recent years has been its tendency to interfere and dominate in politics.

The decade between Roosevelt's 1901 and 1910 speeches (and Wilson's inaugural address in 1911) marked the middle of the Progressive Era in American politics. This was a time of fervent reform, or more accurately, a fervent desire to bring about reforms, in a number of sectors of society: rooting out corruption in politics; providing for the underprivileged; expanding citizen participation; making America a more open, participatory society. And perhaps most central to the Progressive credo, keeping the corporate sector, and the wealthy aristocracy it spawned, in check. As president, Woodrow Wilson marveled at the pace of change and elaborated on the need for firm action in a platform he labeled The New Freedom:

> We are in the presence of a new organization of society. Our life has broken away from the past. The life of America is not the life that it was twenty years ago; it is not the life that it was ten years ago. We have changed our economic conditions, absolutely, from top to bottom; and, with our economic society, the organization of our life.

The most substantial element of that change? The emergence of the modern corporation:

> We have come upon a very different age from any that preceded us. We have come upon an age when we do not do business in the way in which we used to do business,—when we do not carry on any of the operations of manufacture, sale, transportation, or communication as men used to carry them on. There is a sense in which in our day the individual has been submerged. In most parts of our country men work, not for themselves, not as partners in the old way in which they used to work, but generally as employees, in a higher or lower grade,—of great corporations.

An emergence not without its problems:

> ...There was a time when corporations played a very minor part in our business affairs, but now they play the chief part, and most men are the servants of corporations...If the corporation is doing the things that it ought not to do, you really have no voice in the matter and must obey the orders, and you have oftentimes with deep mortification to co-operate in the doing of things which you know are against the public interest. Your individuality is swallowed up in the individuality and purpose of a great organization.

Wilson's New Freedom captured the pace of change and the overwhelming sense of both marvel and disruption, sentiments noted by many observers in the same era. A multitude of social, economic, political and intellectual factors gave rise to a strong undercurrent of anti-corporate sentiment at the dawn of the 20th century. An increasing number of citizens were directly impacted by corporations: as employees, as consumers and, to a small but growing degree, as shareholders. They were affected, as well, by their status as ex-employees. Corporations, in true capitalistic form, were putting many workers out of work through the process that the economist Joseph Schumpeter termed "creative destruction" (Schumpeter expanded on the concept as originally introduced by Karl Marx). Whether jobs were lost directly when a factory closed or company went bankrupt, or indirectly as assembly-line work supplied goods formerly made at home or in small mom and pop business, corporations took the blame.

Social philosophers and muckraking authors took it upon themselves to expose the corporate underbelly. Henry George's 1879 treatise, *Progress and Poverty: An Inquiry into the Cause of Industrial Depressions and of Increase of Want with Increase of Wealth: The Remedy*, quickly became a bestseller in the United States and internationally, second only to the bible in overall sales. Though not focused on corporations per se, George's work brought attention to the social issue of income inequality and the paradox of extreme poverty in a land of plenty.

Other authors focused even more directly on corporate America. Upton Sinclair's The Jungle (1906) alerted the public to the hardships of workers and dangers to consumers from adulterated products; Ida Tarbell's exposé of Standard Oil painted a picture of unfair practices and market manipulations. Ambrose Bierce, as a journalist, wrote scathing articles about the undue political influence of the railroads. Louis Brandeis, prior to his appointment to the Supreme Court, wrote an expose on the banking sector, *Other People's Money and How the Bankers Use It,* with chapter titles like "Our Financial Oligarchy" and "A Curse of Bigness." Labor organizers, whether middle-of-the-roaders like Samuel Gompers or more radicalized agitators like Mother Jones, stirred the pot in an effort to put the labor movement on equal footing with corporate powerbrokers.

Even for those who were not directly impacted as employees, competitors or investors, there were issues that simply rubbed the wrong way. The emergence of the ultra-wealthy class had the unpalatable appearance of an American aristocracy; Carnegie was clearly comfortable with the palaces of the wealthy, but few seemed to share his complacency. The hardship of assembly-line life, ten or more hours a day, six days a week, was dehumanizing, even to those spared from such hardship. Woodrow Wilson wrote that the "individual has been submerged" by corporations employing thousands or hundreds of thousands of men. Tales of pervasive corruption—of bankers and industrialists and lobbyists and judges and politicians making backroom deals and buying favors that benefited everyone but the little guy—filled the newspapers and magazines. Cartoonists like Thomas Nast had a field day.

Anti-corporate sentiment was certainly not new. As we noted earlier, early corporations were resented in England, and reviled in revolutionary America. Modern day anti-corporatism continues a thread of public sentiment that has waxed and waned over the centuries, but never quite disappeared. At the dawn of the 20th century in America, it crested in a wave that ushered in an era of corporate regulation.

CHAPTER 4

CORPORATE REGULATION

The giant trading companies of the 17th century were hard to distinguish from the governments that chartered them. The giant corporate trusts that dominated the economic landscape in the late 19th and early 20th century were a different sort of creature. Chartered by individual states, their relation to the federal government was unclear. Brought into being through general charters, they operated with little restriction or oversight. Their influence on economic life was enormous—seen by some as enormously positive and by others as an enormous threat. They were clearly both, and society sought mechanisms for bringing corporations to heel without killing the goose that laid the golden egg. In the U.S., this effort began with the railroads.

There is quite possibly nothing in modern technology that can serve as an appropriate analogy to the role of the railroads in the late 1800s and early 1900s. We are accustomed to alternatives in the modern age. Trains or trucks or airplanes or ships to move goods; cable or satellite or phone lines for Internet service. But at the turn of the 20th century, railroads were pretty much the sole means of moving large quantities of goods and people over the long East-West corridors of the United States. Boats served coastal and river port cities and towns fairly effectively, but even there, transportation from, say, New York to San Francisco meant a months-long trip around South America—a notoriously turbulent and treacherous sea voyage. Trains made the journey in days.

The presence of a railroad station could bring an economic boom to a community while the discontinuance of a line could just as easily bring a town to ruin. Proximity to a rail line meant farmers could send their output to cities near and far, merchants could carry out long-distance transactions, factories could bring in raw materials and move their finished products. A rise in rail rates meant any business shipping freight had to swallow hard and accept the increased costs, as viable alternatives ranged from infrequent to non-existent.

Figure 4-1: The railroads were early targets of corporate regulation

By its very nature, a great deal of the railroading business was monopolistic. Creating the infrastructure needed for a rail line was extremely capital intensive, and was legally and politically complex, as the lines crossed multiple state and local jurisdictions and required powers of eminent domain to secure the necessary rights of way. The process of connecting two points by rail was not likely to be undertaken more than once, except for select routes between major population centers. The railroads could charge what they pleased and raise rates on a whim—at least, they were largely perceived by the public as doing so. Collusion between lines that did compete (in principle, at least) compounded the situation. The creation of complex trusts that controlled all aspects of rail freight—including transportation services to and from rail lines and warehousing of goods before and after shipping—added to both the reality and the perception that the rails could do what they pleased.

Many railroads offered sharp discounts and rebates to their largest customers, setting up a multi-tiered system of charges that left the small business person and general public at the bottom. Early in 1872, the Pennsylvania Railroad posted an increase in freight costs that doubled the prevailing rates for all shippers…except Standard Oil and a handful of other influential businesses. The announcement was met with rioting, angry newspaper articles and an attempt to boycott Standard Oil's business. The vituperation was so pronounced that John D. Rockefeller began sleeping with a loaded pistol at hand.

Farmers were particularly hard hit. Farms along rail lines that had no competition from other railroads, or from barge traffic, were charged much higher (and less predictable) rates than farmers along competitive routes. The prices charged had little relationship to the actual cost of providing services or the distance goods were transported. The Grange Movement of the 1860s onwards established farmers' cooperatives, in part, to pressure the railroads and the political establishment into a fairer price structure and greater stability of prices and services.

To make matters worse, the rails wooed local officials and national politicians with free transportation in specially-built luxury cars, sweetheart stock deals and other favors, further alienating the general public. In 1882, William Vanderbilt, the New York railroad magnate, son of Cornelius, and, at the time the wealthiest man in the world, responded to a reporter's query about the public interest with the comment "the public be damned". The quote—said by some to be quite uncharacteristic of the man—nevertheless shot around the world. Newspapers, sermonizers, cartoonists, editorial writers, orators all had a field day with the material, dubbing the quote "The Millionaire's Motto" and the "Four Fatal Words". Indeed, William V. is remembered these days for little else.

The public antipathy towards monopolies, Robber Barons, price-fixing, and political chicanery focused on the railroads and led to a general clamor for regulation. The emergent labor movement in America was looking for leverage as well. The Great Railroad Strike of 1877 had shut down much of rail traffic in the eastern U.S. in a strike over wage cuts. The action had not only pitted workers against the rail lines but against the federal troops called in by President Hayes to restore rail traffic. In the strike's aftermath, labor hoped to reverse the tide, and bring the authority of the federal government into its own corner, or at least, to strike a better balance.

The Federal Government Steps In

The Supreme Court, in the Wabash Case of 1886, limited the authority of the states to regulate railroads with an interstate presence, thereby forcing a stark choice: the federal government could either regulate the railroads, or adopt a complete hands-off policy under which neither the federal nor state governments played any significant oversight role. The political climate of the day gave rise to the first significant U.S. effort at federal corporate regulation, The Interstate Commerce Act of 1887, a law aimed at controlling prices and practices in the rail industry.

The railroads were not totally opposed to federal oversight. Although they frequently operated in a near-monopolistic manner, they were also buffeted by other near-monopolies. The insistence of their largest clients (like Standard Oil) to ship product at unrealistically low rates meant that railroads had to operate some lines and services at a loss, and scrounge for profits from less influential customers. In essence, the smaller businesses were subsidizing the giant corporate trusts of the day.

Federal price regulation could bring order to what were otherwise chaotic railroad pricing schemes, a prospect that was welcome by some of the railroad companies, at least. Although they were less sanguine about other provisions of proposed legislation, their objections were not enough to vigorously oppose federal regulatory authority. The Interstate Commerce Act gave the federal government broad authority to regulate prices in the rail industry for any rail traffic that crossed state lines. The government did not try to set prices, per se, but required prices to be "just and reasonable" and exerted control over how industry pricing would work. Rail lines were required to publish their fares, which had to be the same for large customers and small. Distance was now factored into pricing: short haul fares could not be more expensive than long haul fares on the same line. And the act created the first federal agency aimed at regulating industry—the Interstate Commerce Commission. The ICC would serve as a model for federal regulatory agencies yet to come.

America was not the only country to recognize and respond to the role of the railroad as critical national infrastructure and a vital component of the economy. Other countries—France, Austria, Italy, Germany (Prussia), Japan and Canada, for example—nationalized their rail services to bring them under the government's umbrella (nationalization was considered, on and off, in the U.S. as well and was temporarily imposed during World War I). Britain passed the Regulation of Railways Act in 1873, creating a special tribunal to hear cases regarding unfair practices and pricing schemes in the rail industry; commissioners of the tribunal were required to divest themselves of all financial holdings in the railroads.

It's not our intent to offer a detailed history of the regulation of railroads but to simply point to the creation of the ICC as the beginning of an era of federal regulation of industry in the U.S. Some of the factors leading to such regulation were specific to the railroads, particularly the combination of the essential nature of the industry and discriminatory pricing practices that frustrated its users. The railroads were seen as a public good—weren't the lands ceded for their use public lands, after all? Other factors were more generalized: the burgeoning labor movement; resentment of an apparent American aristocracy of Carnegies, Rockefellers and Vanderbilts; numerous social justice movements; anti-monopolists; political corruption; muckraking journalism. In fairly rapid succession, the ICC was followed by other laws expanding regulation of the railroads, clarifying the authorities of the ICC and extending jurisdiction to other sectors.

The Railroad Safety Appliance Act (1893) extended ICC authority to railroad safety. The full title of the law is unusually descriptive: *An Act to Promote the Safety of Employees and Travelers upon Railroads by Compelling Common Carriers Engaged in Interstate Commerce to Equip Their Cars with Automatic Couplers and Continuous Brakes and Their Locomotives with Driving-wheel Brakes, and for Other Purposes.* Amendments in 1903 and 1910 strengthened ICC safety oversight even further. The 1910 Mann-Elkins Act clarified the ICC's rate-oversight authority (which had been called into question by several court cases) and more significantly, expanded ICC authority beyond railroads to include telephone and telegraph companies, setting the stage for what would one day become the Federal Radio Commission and eventually the Federal

Communications Commission. The Valuation Act (1913) made the ICC the official arbiter of corporate valuations for the railroads, a factor in setting rates.

In fairly rapid succession, the ICC was followed by other laws expanding regulation of the railroads, clarifying the authorities of the ICC and extending jurisdiction to other sectors. The Railroad Safety Appliance Act (1893) extended ICC authority to railroad safety. Amendments in 1903 and 1910 strengthened ICC safety oversight even further. The 1910 Mann-Elkins Act clarified the ICC's rate-oversight authority (which had been called into question by several court cases) and more significantly, expanded ICC authority beyond railroads to include telephone and telegraph companies, setting the stage for what would one day become the Federal Radio Commission and eventually the Federal Communications Commission. The Valuation Act (1913) made the ICC the official arbiter of corporate valuations for the railroads, a factor in setting rates.

Numerous laws were passed providing a federal role for resolving the fractious and often violent disputes that arose between railroad labor and management. The Arbitration Act of 1888 authorized a panel to resolve disputes through non-binding recommendations, but the toothless law resulted in only a single panel convening in response to the 1894 Pullman Strike; by the time the panel actually met, the strike had been resolved. The Erdman Act of 1898 also relied on a non-binding arbitration mechanism, but added significant protections to railroad workers, especially a provision prohibiting companies from banning union activity as a condition of employment. The Newlands Act of 1913 added additional mediation provisions. Perhaps most significant to the labor movement was the passage of the Adamson Act in 1916, which mandated an 8-hour day for rail employees without any reduction in salary, and with additional pay for overtime. This was the first instance of federal law regulating worker hours in private industry.

The federal government did not restrict itself to railroads. Theodore Roosevelt signed into law the Pure Food and Drug Act of 1906 as well as the Federal Meat Inspection Act in the same year, both laws following quickly the publication of Upton Sinclair's exposé, *The Jungle* (the book published in 1906, was published the year before as serialized articles in *Appeal to Reason*, a Socialist newspaper). The laws were part of the "three C's" of Roosevelt's "Square Deal"—conservation, consumer protection, and corporate regulation. Other laws emerged. The 16th Amendment to the Constitution, passed in 1909, allowed for the collection of income taxes from individuals as well as from corporations. The Federal Trade Commission Act of 1914 intended to shine a governmental spotlight on unfair and deceptive business practices.

All major pieces of legislation, no matter how popular the cause, are bound to elicit some opposition. One exception to this general rule—perhaps the most well-supported bill in the history of Congress—was passed unanimously in the House and with only a single dissenting vote in the Senate. Signed into law in 1890 by President Benjamin Harrison, the act reflected the enormous degree of public concern and sheer antipathy that was directed at the monopolistic trusts of the day. The law was the Sherman Antitrust Act.

Sherman Antitrust Act

Senator John Sherman came from an accomplished Ohio family. One brother was a federal judge, a second brother was a prominent banker and a third the famous Civil War general, William Tecumseh Sherman. Charles Sherman, the boys' father, was a justice on the Ohio Supreme Court. John Sherman served three terms in the House of Representatives before accepting a vacated seat in the United States Senate. He was appointed Secretary of the Treasury by President Rutherford B. Hayes, then returned to the Senate in 1880 until becoming Secretary of State in 1897 under President William McKinley. In the process, he ran for president three times.

On March 21, 1890, Sherman gave an extended speech on the floor of the Senate (which he begins by proclaiming that he hadn't intended to make any extended remarks), where—as politicians are wont to do—he explains the rationale for a bill he sponsored and defends its provisions. The bill would eventually pass into law and become known to history as the Sherman Antitrust Act. His remarks focus on the issues that brought antitrust to the fore and provide insight to the depth of feelings underlying the legislation.

First, of course, are the trusts themselves. They are no run-of-the-mill policy issue for the Senators to consider. Sherman asks, rhetorically, "Do I exaggerate the evil we have to deal with? I do not think so." He is careful to elucidate the benefits of industrial enterprise, no matter what its scale of activity, as long as there is healthy competition in play. But trusts that quash competition are another matter:

> These trusts and combinations are great wrongs to the people. They have invaded many of the most important branches of business. They operate with a double-edged sword. They increase beyond reason the cost of the necessaries of life and business, and they decrease the cost of the raw material, the farm products of the country. They regulate prices at their will, depress the price of what they buy and increase the price of what they sell. They aggregate to themselves great, enormous wealth by extortion which makes the people poor. Then, making this extorted wealth the means of further extortion from their unfortunate victims…they pursue unmolested, unrestrained by law, their ceaseless round of peculation under the law, till they are fast producing that condition on our people in which the great mass of them are the servitors of those who have this aggregated wealth at their command.

Ignoring the excesses of corporate trusts, Sherman warns, is to invite excess of another kind. Monopolistic greed, if not constrained, will invite a severe societal backlash from "the socialist, the communist, and the nihilist. Society is now disturbed by forces never felt before." Unless the trusts are reigned in, Sherman suggests, dissent and anarchy will threaten America's very foundation.

Who are these corporate extortionists? "I do not wish to single out any particular trust," Sherman informs his colleagues, and then promptly goes on to single out several:

- Standard Oil, for not only crushing competition, but for compelling a railroad to lower the prices charged to Standard Oil to 10 cents a barrel, raise the prices charged to a competitor to 35 cents a barrel, and then requiring the railroad *to pay* Standard Oil the 25 cents a barrel difference.
- The Chicago Gas-Light and Coke Company, and The People's Gas-Light and Coke Company, for agreeing to divide the city into non-competitive territories, thereby keeping the price of gas artificially high.
- Grain dealers in Illinois
- "[T]he cotton trust, the whiskey trust, the sugar refiner's trust, the cotton-baggers trust, the copper trust, the salt trust, and many others" of which Senator Sherman felt the public was already well aware.

Sherman also takes to task the Diamond Match Company, an enterprise we will revisit in a later chapter, noting that "the supply of the article and the price thereof are made to depend upon the action of a half-dozen individuals...to satisfy their cupidity and avarice...regardless of the wants and necessities of over sixty millions of people..":

> ...The Diamond Match Company was organized for the purpose of controlling the manufacture and trade in matches in the United States and Canada. The object was to get all the manufacturers of matches...to enter into a combination and agreement, by which...all match factories should be controlled by the Diamond Match Company. …The article thus completely under their control...has come to be regarded as one of necessity, not only in every household in the land, but one of daily use by almost every individual...It is difficult to conceive of a monopoly which can affect a greater number of people...Indeed, it is doubtful if free government can long exist in a country where such enormous amounts of money are allowed to be accumulated in the vaults of corporations, to be used at discretion in controlling the property and business of the country...

Several of the examples Sherman cited came from state court cases, where the allegations involved collusion that occurred totally (or mostly) within a single state. Indeed, many states had already enacted antitrust legislation, and some of these laws served as models for the bill Sherman introduced. State laws were limited in their ability to affect interstate operations, however, which brings us to the second issue motivating national attention.

The country had grown! Industry had grown. Railroads, telegraphs, canals and the sheer size of the American economy had facilitated business arrangements that crossed state borders more or less willy-nilly. The United States had become, as Sherman put it, "…a continental empire of forty-two States." No government entity below the federal level could take effective action to reign in trusts (if, indeed, they needed reigning in…there were those in 1890, and those now, who would disagree). Congress needed to act, if for no other reason than as a sign of the maturing and expanding role of the federal government.

To drive home the dangers of inaction, Sherman's final example of a specific trust was of one being formed, as he described it…

> "…to affect the price of silver bullion...It will enable a few corporations... to corner the Government of the United States in its proposed effort...to purchase silver bullion as the basis and security for paper money. Can

> anyone doubt that such a combination is unlawful, against public policy, with power enough to control the operation of your laws, and destructive to all competition...?"

His point is clear. With the very money supply of the United States at stake, how can Congress do anything but take steps to prevent corporations from the excesses of influence and control that they exercise when combined into trusts. Trusts are "evil", effect "almost every individual" in the land and threaten the very existence of "free government." As we noted, the bill passed with near unanimity in both houses of Congress. To the best of our knowledge, no major piece of federal legislation has since enjoyed such overwhelming support.

The law itself, though, was not nearly as clear-cut as the sentiment behind it, and implementation of the Sherman Antitrust Act got off to a rocky start. Lacking a straightforward definition of "trust", courts were left to glean the meaning of the law on their own, and decisions were readily subject to challenge. An 1895 Supreme Court case, United States v. E. C. Knight Company, was the first to bring the Sherman Antitrust Act before the highest court, regarding creation of a sugar trust that controlled 98 percent of U.S. production. The court found the trust was not in violation of the Sherman Antitrust Act on the grounds that manufacturing did not, in itself, fall under the umbrella of "interstate commerce," since manufacturing is an inherently local activity. The decision greatly weakened application of the law. Another Supreme Court case held that the antitrust law applied to labor unions as well as business corporations, further steering the law in directions unanticipated by Senator Sherman.

The Sherman Antitrust Act—eventually clarified and strengthened by various revisions and court cases—still stands today as the major antitrust statute in the United States. It has been used to challenge modern corporate giants such as AT&T (which was actually dismantled) and Microsoft and has levied fines of $100 million or more against dozens of companies for monopolistic practices, including:

- Hoffmann-La Roche regarding the price of vitamins
- Bridgestone, for specialized rubber products for tires
- LG for LCD panels
- Samsung for memory chips
- Archer Daniels Midland for food ingredients

- Several passenger and freight airlines, including British Airways, Korean Air, and Air France

The March of Legislation

The late-19th century efforts to regulate the railroads and then, more broadly, to legislate against corporate trusts marked the beginning of the growth in the authority of the federal government to impose its will on corporate practices deemed contrary to the public good. Corporations were no longer constrained by their charters, as they had been for hundreds of years. Interstate business operations, by their very nature, could not be effectively regulated by individual states. Although the political appetite for corporate regulation waxed and waned in different eras and under different administrations, the general trend has been an increase in regulatory oversight throughout the 20th century, a trend that has continued into the 21st century, although not without considerable challenges as to the wisdom of regulatory efforts.

Some of the major regulatory touchstones during the Progressive Era—roughly between the creation of the Interstate Commerce Commission and the outbreak of World War I—are in the table 4-1:

LAW	YEAR	PRESIDENT	PURPOSE
Interstate Commerce	1887	Cleveland	Restrict preferential pricing in railroad industry; create the Interstate Commerce Commission
Sherman Anti-Trust	1890	Harrison	Prevent and if needed, break up monopolies
Harter Act	1893	Harrison	Regulate liability and contracts for water shipping companies
Safety Appliance	1893	Harrison	Railroad safety law
Erdman Act	1898	McKinley	Required arbitration of railroad labor disputes
Rivers and Harbor Act	1899	McKinley	Prohibit dumping of wastes that obstruct navigation
Elkins Act	1903	T. Roosevelt	Expanded ICC authority to levy fines
Hepburn Act	1906	T. Roosevelt	Further expansion of ICC and addition of pipeline oversight
Pure Food and Drug	1906	T. Roosevelt	First major food industry safety law
Meat Inspection	1906	T. Roosevelt	Meat safety and truth-in-labeling act

Ash Pan	1908	T. Roosevelt	Additional railroad safety measures
Corporate Income Tax	1909	Taft	Excise tax on corporate income; superseded by the 16th Amendment in 1913
Mann-Elkins Act	1910	Taft	Extended ICC authority to telecommunications
Boiler Inspection	1911	Taft	Railroad safety measures
Phosphorus Match Act	1912	Taft	First federal control of a dangerous industrial substance
Department of Labor Act	1913	Taft/Wilson	Taft signed a law on the last day of his administration, creating the cabinet-level Department of Labor
Federal Reserve Act	1913	Wilson	Required US-chartered banks to be part of newly-formed federal reserve system
Federal Trade Commiss.	1914	Wilson	Created the FTC to assure truthful advertising claims
Clayton Antitrust	1914	Wilson	Clarified meaning of 'trusts' and expanded authority over them
Seamen's Act	1915	Wilson	Regulated working conditions for merchant seamen
Child Labor Act	1916	Wilson	Restricted use of children in the workplace
Adamson Act	1916	Wilson	Established 8-hour workday for railroad workers
Federal Employees	1916	Wilson	Early form of workers' compensation for federal employees injured on the job
Esch-Cummins Act	1920	Wilson	Returned railroads to private operation after WWI, but with new regulatory controls

Table 4-1: Major US Corporate Laws of the Progressive Era

The political appetite for corporate regulation waxed and waned in different eras and under different administrations. Warren Harding was not inclined to champion new regulation, though he more or less browbeat the steel industry into accepting the by-then common 8-hour day for its workers. The Coolidge administration's program of business regulation was characterized by one biographer as "thin to the point of invisibility." It took the Great Depression and Franklin Roosevelt's New Deal to return business regulation to the forefront of the public policy agenda. Roosevelt's initiatives included passage of the Glass-Stegall Act (banking), establishment of a federal minimum wage, creation of both the

Securities and Exchange Commission and the Federal Communications Commission, passage of the National Industrial Recovery Act to regulate industry and the National Labor Relations Act to put labor unions on more equal footing with corporations during worker-management negotiations.

Environmental Regulation to the Forefront

The social upheaval of the 1970's ushered in the next—and very substantial—era of regulatory oversight for American business. When the Cuyahoga River in Ohio caught fire in 1969 from an accumulation of industrial oil and grease discharges—broadcast on television throughout the US and around the world—the public sentiment seemed to be "Enough!" It was not the first time a waterway had gone up in flames, but the dramatic images of the Cuyahoga burning, coupled with the growing awareness of other environmental issues—from smog-choked cities and contaminated drinking water, to poisoned communities in Minimata, Japan and Love Canal, New York, to workplace cancers and the DDT-endangered status of the bald eagle—created enormous societal momentum for change.

As was the case in the Progressive Era, passionate exposes, like Rachel Carson's 1962 masterwork, Silent Spring, played an important role in galvanizing public sentiment. Big factories, with their belching smokestacks and open discharge pipes, became not only the obvious targets for regulations, but the most straightforward means of achieving rapid reductions in pollution. And since pollution was notoriously disrespectful of human-drawn boundaries, state laws, once again, were not considered particularly useful in addressing large-scale environmental concerns. Federal action was called for.

Passage of major environmental laws happened in quick succession: The National Environmental Policy Act in 1969, the Clean Air Act (1970), Occupational Safety and Health Act (1970), Lead Paint Act (1970), the Clean Water Act (1972), Federal Insecticide, Fungicide and Rodenticide Act (1972), Endangered Species Act (1973), Oil Pollution Act (1973), Safe Drinking Water Act (1974), Resource Conservation and Recovery Act (hazardous wastes - 1976), Toxic Substances and Control Act (1976), and the Comprehensive Environmental Response, Compensation and Liability Act (Superfund - 1980). President Nixon also created the U.S. Environmental Protection Agency by Executive Order in 1970.

It was a busy decade. Environmental laws imposed a type of regulatory oversight that was, in several respects, far more intrusive than earlier anti-monopoly, financial, labor and safety laws. The new round of laws required companies to obtain operational permits not just at the corporate level, but for each individual facility. The permits often regulated individual pieces of equipment—each vent, tank or stack that was a significant source of air emissions; each pipe discharging to public waters or to sewage treatment plants; each shipment of hazardous wastes. Companies were required to test, document and report on their pollution levels, and to open their facility gates to an array of national, state and local inspectors. In a rarely used legal maneuver, liability was made retroactive, so that corporations in the current era could be held responsible for cleaning up contaminated hazardous waste sites created long before the Superfund law was passed.

The steady drumbeat of new environmental legislation in the 1970s slowed in subsequent decades without ever coming to a full halt. The Superfund amendments of 1986 not only strengthened the Superfund program, but added novel reporting requirements—community right-to-know programs—that made information on facility handling of toxic chemicals widely available to the public. Air, water and solid waste laws were updated, sometimes with substantial new programs, and safety-related regulations were expanded regarding food safety, oil transportation, nuclear energy, pesticides, and consumer products.

Technological and Social Drivers

In addition to the environmental agenda, other social issues drove new regulations for corporations. The Civil Rights Act of 1964 and President Johnson's Executive Order on affirmative action (1965) imposed additional requirements and restrictions on how business could do business. Anti-discrimination laws profoundly affected business hiring habits and employee accommodations. Ralph Nader's 1965 book, Unsafe at Any Speed, shone a spotlight on automotive safety (or the lack thereof), with a consequent increase in rules for auto manufacturers. Whistleblower rules protected employees who revealed illegal company and contractor activity, even offering *qui tam* rewards in some cases.

Various financial upheavals such as the savings and loan crisis of the 1980s and the subprime mortgage crisis that began in earnest in 2007-2008 led to a number of new legislative programs regulating the banking and securities industries. Scandals in insider trading, offshore tax havens, and corporate tax inversion strategies have also led to additional regulations and calls for even more. Regulations have an international reach. U.S. companies are prohibited from paying bribes to secure overseas business, and are required to report their use of certain "conflict minerals" that are mined in foreign lands under harsh conditions to benefit warring parties.

A slew of anti-money-laundering and know-your-customer have changed the way banks and securities companies do business. AML/KYC rules, as they're known in the business, are designed to make it much more difficult than in the past for illegal entities such as drug cartels and terrorist organizations to move cash through the financial system.

The burgeoning importance of the Internet has led to a slew of regulatory approaches to both empower and restrict corporate activities in this arena. Due to the inherently global nature of networked electronic communications, laws in one jurisdiction can have an outsized influence. The European General Data Protection Regulation, implemented in 2018, protects the privacy of those in EU countries who visit websites that may collect information on the visitor. But since a European can easily visit sites in other countries, and non-Europeans can visit sites in Europe, the law's reach has led to global-scale retrenching of privacy rules on millions of websites in scores of countries.

The abandonment of net neutrality policy in the United States, also in 2018, means that Internet giants like Google, Amazon and Verizon are now treated less like tightly-regulated utilities and can adopt pricing and transmission strategies that favor some customers over others. Copyright and trademark laws have been revamped around the world to make it easier for the likes of corporations to protect their intellectual property online. Rupert Murdoch once referred to search engines like Google as "content kleptomaniacs"; revised copyright laws make it easier for Murdoch and other publishers to protect their content.

Privacy concerns have also given rise to regulations impacting Internet services. The so-called *right to be forgotten* is considered a fundamental human right in Europe and requires online firms like Google to, under certain conditions, remove content from their search results that individuals don't want to be associated with. A legal case in Spain, for example, required Google to remove one person's records regarding his foreclosure history from the search results on the person's name.

Ironically, even with the original material now removed, current searches immediately bring up the right-to-be-forgotten case which includes information about the foreclosure.

Security breaches that release data records on millions—sometimes hundreds of millions—of users are also likely to lead to greater regulatory oversight of online services. So too with manipulation of social networking sites, as with the accusation that Russian operators used sites like Facebook and Twitter to actively interfere with elections in the U.S. and other countries. Regulations to address these concerns, if and when they arrive, will be faced with a delicate balance. Users, by the millions and billions, agree to make some personal data available in exchange for the services that Google, Facebook and others provide. The companies, in turn, monetize the data in numerous ways.

What are the limits in using information that may include personal search history, purchasing habits and even political preferences? Some users are horrified to learn that companies amass location data that tracks a user's whereabouts. Others have complained that internet companies don't know *enough* about them and continue, for example, to present pregnancy and new baby advertisements even after a user has told online friends about her miscarriage. Regulators are in fairly uncharted waters when it comes to issues like these.

Regulatory Pros and Cons

It perhaps goes without saying that the corporate world generally prefers to be unregulated rather than regulated and that when regulations are inevitable, to have them applied with a light touch. But businesses are neither unilaterally nor universally opposed to federal regulation. The absence of a federal regulatory structure to address a perceived problem can result in a patchwork of highly-variable state programs that greatly magnify the difficulties of achieving compliance. This is especially the case for disruptive services, like Uber and Airbnb that upend traditional business models and elicit new regulations not only at the state and local level in the U.S., but across the world.

Regulations for some industries create opportunities for others, as is the case with the robust environmental services industry that emerged from the pollution control laws of the 1970s. But corporate regulation also generates significant anti-regulatory sentiment, on the grounds that excessive regulations hold back corporations from their principle role of providing products, generating wealth, and providing jobs. As this book was in progress, the administration of President Trump was embarked on an aggressive program to allow corporations to operate much more freely, with not only fewer regulatory responsibilities, but with a substantially smaller tax burden in the United States. Time will tell how this push will impact the corporate and the natural world. But there are two truths about the regulatory environment that, while perhaps obvious, are worth making explicit.

First, regulations can accomplish precisely the goals they were designed to achieve. This is most obvious in the environmental arena, where readily measurable results can track the trends over time in lowering industrial emissions, improving air and water quality, or lessening the body burden of contaminants like lead or mercury. Safety regulations sometimes have the same type of clear outcomes; there is no doubt that seatbelt regulations have saved lives in a manner that is readily quantifiable. Energy conservation rules have made cars, refrigerators, lightbulbs, furnaces and many other devices much less demanding in terms of their fossil fuel requirements.

Some social regulations, such as requirements in some countries to increase the presence of women on corporate boards, also yield readily observable outcomes. Results can be more difficult to crystallize in other arenas; we likely will never know with any certainty the degree to which the Foreign Corrupt Practices Act has actually minimized corrupt practices, although the fines and prosecutions issued under the law, which are infrequent but often substantial, certainly suggest the U.S. companies will give careful consideration to avoiding practices prohibited by the law.

Second, regulations impose economic costs and provide economic benefits. Often, there is substantial institutional distance between the two. The costs are borne by individual regulated entities and the benefits accrue to the whole of society. The Environmental Protection Agency, for example, estimates that the benefits of the Clean Air Act exceed costs by a factor of thirty to one. Even at the lowest end of the cost-benefit estimates, there's a 3-to-1 return on expenditures. Individual companies pay the costs of pollution control while the savings largely reflect broad societal benefits.

However, even regulated companies can discover surprising benefits to regulatory oversight; companies required to manage their waste streams often find the means to handle their materials with greater overall efficiency and save money in the process (regulations have much in common with competition—neither is welcomed in the corporate world, but both can effectively drive greater productivity). On the other hand, various economists and think tanks have offered estimates suggesting the combined impact of regulation creates an overall drag on the economy that has cost the nation trillions of dollars in lost growth. Though we lean rather strongly in the direction of viewing regulations as beneficial, both to individual firms and to society as a whole, the most conclusive statement we can muster on the overall impacts of regulation is that, from an economic perspective, the jury is still out.

The legal structure imposes its most draconian costs to businesses in the case of egregious violations, assessed directly as administrative fines and or as court-directed settlements. Both the tobacco industry and the asbestos industry were held liable for the deaths and other health impacts caused by their products, impacts that were known within the respective industries but kept hidden from the public. Asbestos was deemed so hazardous that the material has almost totally disappeared from the market. Asbestos manufacturers like Johns-Manville were driven into bankruptcy, and insurers like Lloyds of London, forced to pay billions in asbestos-related damages, came very close to going under, but not before a series of government actions and class action lawsuits created funds to help support those affected by asbestos exposure. In the US, the funds are expected to pay out about $30 billion over time.

The tobacco industry, on the other hand, is still thriving, a financial fact of life made possible by a much broader customer base, despite much larger settlements in this industry. The 1998 Master Settlement Agreement between tobacco companies and state governments in the US has already directed about $100 billion to state coffers (only some of which is used for anti-smoking campaigns) and is expected to total over $200 billion for the first 25 years of the agreement.

It's not just toxic material that can lead to settlements in the hundreds of billions. Toxic mortgages will do just as nicely. The sum total of fines and settlements that have (so far) grown out the subprime mortgage crisis (roughly 2007 to 2010) is in the neighborhood of $240 billion. The fines, labelled as "staggering" in numerous news reports, include $76 billion levied against Bank of America for liabilities largely inherited from its acquisition of Countrywide Mortgage, and $44 billion for JPMorgan Chase, largely for the practice of robosigning mortgages without proper due diligence. Though initiated by regulators in the United States, the reach of the $240 billion in fines was international, including Germany's Deutsche Bank ($14b), Royal Bank of Scotland ($10b), France's BNP Paribas ($9b), and two Swiss banks, Credit Suisse ($49b) and UBS ($6b).

Nor are fines the only consequences. John Varley, CEO of Barclays Bank during the mortgage crisis, is facing charges from the UK government of conspiracy to commit fraud, facing a possible jail sentence of 22 years. Iceland has imprisoned two senior bank executives—a chairman and the bank CEO—for conspiracy to manipulate markets, making them the only country to send senior managers to jail for the violations contributing to the mortgage crisis. The United States, in contrast, convicted more than 300 financial professionals for securities-related crimes, but largely targeted mid-level rather than senior executives.

Other countries issue corporate fines, of course, but none come close to the level of financial punishments issued by the federal government (and often, by states as well) in the United States. The US reputation as both a litigious and regulation-prone society seems well-deserved. But as noted in our earlier discussion of Volkswagen's *Dieselgate* scandal, oversight is generally carried out with a light-enough touch so as to not threaten the overall wellbeing of the company under scrutiny.

Government regulations, by their very nature, are a means of exercising power over the regulated community. Corporations did not cede their authority willingly, nor did they stand idly by without trying to influence regulations directly. When regulations came into effect despite industry efforts to avoid them, they took steps to recover some of their lost authorities through other means. Many people hold the belief—reasonably so—that, government regulations notwithstanding, corporate power has been ascendant in the modern age. We'll explore the expansion of corporate power in Chapter 7. But before we do, it pays to illustrate the growth of a familiar company at a time when corporations in the U.S. were on their way to becoming national, and then global, behemoths.

CHAPTER 5

DIAMOND MATCH

A late nineteenth, early twentieth century businessman with the unlikely name of Ohio Columbus Barber was an industrialist whose business empire had a depth and a reach that was quite possibly more extensive than any other of his era. Everyone was familiar with Barber's products and most people in the United States used them on a daily basis as did a sizable fraction of the world's population.

At his peak, his companies owned vast tracts of the natural landscape, had a labor force of thousands, introduced technological and marketing innovations at a breathtaking pace, operated their own farms, towns and railroad lines, cornered intellectual property, wooed governments and journalists, manipulated stock trading, and thoroughly crushed any competition. Those he could not beat by providing a superior product at a competitive price he undercut by lowering his prices below cost, strangled distribution channels so that others could not bring their product to market, or simply bought whole companies outright and abandoned them, rather than face them in the open market.

Not content with a domestic monopoly, Barber travelled widely in search of international sources for new markets, launching operations in over a dozen countries around the globe. His goal was to see his products in use in every U.S. home and as his empire grew, in every home in every industrialized country. He introduced a brand known to all in 19th century America, a brand that remained a household name throughout the 20th and into the 21st centuries.

If Barber himself is not well known, it is probably because his product was so pedestrian. Rockefeller's riches came from the oil that powered the global economy; Vanderbilt operated the marvelous steamships and railroads that moved people and goods; Carnegie built magnificent, fearsome steel mills. O.C. Barber made matches. Billions and billions of matches.

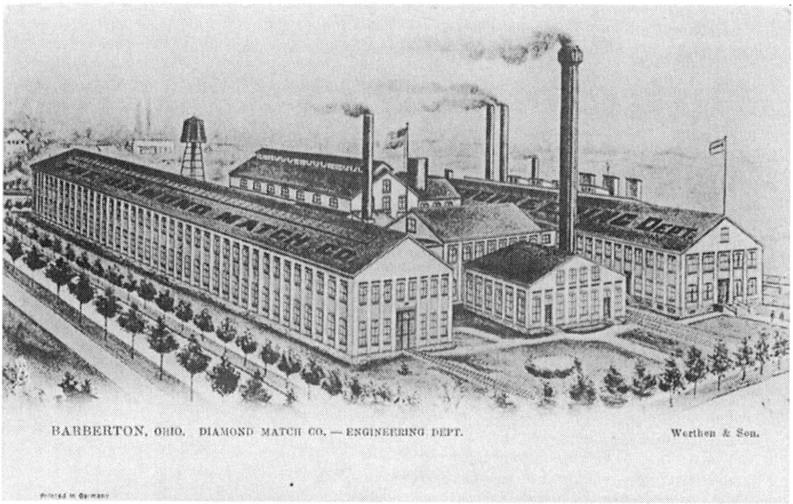

Figure 5-1: The Diamond Match Co. factory in Barberton, Ohio

Until the early 1800's, a person who wanted to start a flame had to use essentially the same techniques as his ancestors did 1,000 centuries earlier, when *Homo sapiens* first mastered fire. The process was strictly mechanical, required two objects, and involved either rubbing them fast enough and furiously enough to produce frictional heat or striking them together in hopes they'd produce enough of a spark to get a fire going (concentrating the sun's rays with a magnifying glass, was an infrequently-used third method that came much later in history).

In either case, the procedure was laborious enough, and uncertain enough, that a good deal of ordinary life prior to the mid-1800s revolved around maintaining a more or less perpetual fire. New candles were lit before old ones were extinguished; tapers were ignited from lanterns; coals in stoves and embers in hearths were piled up for the night and tended early the next morning in order to restart a robust fire. A home without a fire could not cook, could not heat water for bathing, could not warm a room and—horror of horrors—could not light a pipe or cigar for an evening smoke. When a fire was lost, it was often easier to visit a neighbor for a few hot coals than it was to start a new fire from scratch.

Technology hadn't stood still for 100,000 years, of course. Instead of striking two stones together, a 19th century gentlemen carried a tinder box containing iron and flint to make a spark, a piece of shredded textile or other combustible materials to nurse the spark into a flame, and perhaps a pellet of sulfur that could also be ignited by the smallest of flames. At some point, someone had the clever idea of mixing the sulfur with beeswax or gum arabic and molding it onto a small stick—a match. But this was still a match that was lit by laborious means. The quick-lighting chemical match was yet to appear.

Chemists and experimenters of the era had identified several materials that easily ignited with only the slightest encouragement. Tinkerers began to modify the composition of the tinder box match with the aim of creating matches that would light more quickly and reliably without the need for creating a spark or for prolonged and vigorous action to create friction. The earliest matches appeared around 1800 and were cumbersome, dangerous affairs that required crushing a small vial of sulfuric acid to start the chemical reaction necessary to light the match. Wooden friction matches, like those that are familiar to us today, made a tentative appearance a few decades later.

At its outset, match manufacturing was a small scale, cottage industry with each tinkerer relying on their own formula and match-making techniques. The matches were generally unreliable and dangerous. Manufacturers experimented with matches that could be lit on any rough surface and those that needed to be struck on a special material to initiate a flame. They went by a wide variety of names: friction lights, percussion matches, safety matches, loco focos, lucifers, fuzees, vestas, Vesuvians, flamers, wind matches, candle matches, parlor matches and even a specialized drunkard's match designed to burn only half-way down the splint, so as not to endanger the fingers of an inattentive user.

Regardless of the name, these matches, too, were generally unreliable and dangerous. Sufficient friction was needed that early friction matches came packaged with a piece of sandpaper, and the match was lit by folding the sandpaper over the match, grasping the match head, and giving a sharp pull. The failure rate was high, with the match refusing to light or, quite often, the head flying off because of the effort involved. A successful light was typically accompanied by a multitude of sparks in all directions, errant flames, and sharp, sulfuric odors. Individual matches were dangerous enough, but shipped in bulk, the products were positively deadly. Cartons of matches jostled by bumpy transportation were prone to bursting into flame or exploding outright. Railroads refused to carry the product in any quantity, so manufacturers had to transport matches by horse-drawn carriage, greatly limiting the opportunities for distribution.

As formulas and techniques improved, manufacturers strove to produce matches with minimal sparks, non-offensive odors, long-lasting flames, and matches that could function even in windy or moist conditions. At a time when the average household had very little in the way of *technology*—no electric lighting, no powered appliances, no motorized transportation, no communication devices—matches began to make an appearance as one of the first truly modern household conveniences.

Ohio's father, George Barber was one of these early makers of matches. He set up operations in his Middlebury, Ohio barn in 1845, when commercial match-making was barely a decade old. Barber made block matches by cutting grooves tic-tac-toe style into square blocks of wood, so that 64 or 81 or 100 match-sized splints remained. He mixed a blend of chemicals that he concocted on his own to coat the match tips, dipped, dried, and packaged the blocks, and sold the final product. Users would break a match off from the block as needed.

Ohio Columbus joined his father's small business and became its key salesman. His biographers describe him as a man of true entrepreneurial qualities: an enormous drive to succeed; a single-minded commitment that placed business above all else; a personality both charming and forceful that cajoled or intimidated others to see things his way. Most of all, O.C. Barber, as he was known to his associates (he was Hi to his friends) had a vision. He understood that a reliable, affordable match would become a household essential and that billions of matches would be needed every year. He recognized the larger forces at work—railroads, communications, science, patents, financing—that would escalate match manufacturing from a piecemeal backyard business to a large-scale, technologically sophisticated industry.

The Barber Match Company grew into a solidly thriving business in the Akron area and by the 1860's, George and O.C. Barber acquired industrial operations along the Cuyahoga River to accommodate production of both block matches and newly-designed stick matches. The company expanded into related activities, such as making and printing the boxes that held the finished matches. Barber Match employed about 20 workers. The Civil War increased demand even further—matches were issued to Union soldiers—and Ohio Columbus opted to stay with the business even as most of his compatriots went off to fight for the Union cause.

By 1870, Barber Match had about 70 workers on its payroll. It competed with four other match companies in Ohio and about 80 companies nationwide. Competition between firms was fierce and the industry landscape shifted dramatically in the next decade. By 1880, Barber Match was the only Ohio match manufacturer remaining—one of 37 in the country—and was producing about 20 percent of the nation's total. A decade later, O.C. Barber would found his own eponymous company town, Barberton, Ohio, to house his rapidly growing business.

The success of the Barber Match Company did not come easily. Profit margins (when such were to be had) were slim and technological changes came rapidly, continually upending the business. O.C. Barber was constantly on the lookout for new chemistries, new machines, new production methods and new patents—innovations in any area—that could give his company a competitive edge. Barber's was one of the first companies to add electric lights in his factories, enabling a night shift and increasing overall production. Barber Match developed a premium line of sulfur-free matches to eliminate the unpleasant brimstone odors. Mixtures were modified in an attempt to bond the matchhead more securely to the splint, to make the match more moisture resistant, or to improve other features of the product's safety and reliability. Improvements were not limited to manufacturing, but focused on other channels of business, such as labor relations, distribution and marketing. Barber's installation of an employee cafeteria—a rarity in his day—was met with cheers by his labor force and glowing mentions in the Akron press.

Innovations begat opportunities. Barber had a recently-invented sprinkler system installed in his factory in the hopes of preventing the sort of ruinous fires that had destroyed several other Ohio businesses. He was so impressed with the operation of the system that he joined forces with the sprinkler's inventor and formed a company to market the device to others; the company eventually became the Grinnell Corporation, which exists to this day as a subsidiary of Tyco International. Barber Match needed large supplies of paper to box and label its product, so O.C. Barber went into the paper business as well. At various times he was president or a key executive of the National Sewer Pipe Co,. the Creedmoor Cartridge Co., the American Alumina Co., the Barber Whiteware Co., the Kirkham Art Tile and Pottery Co., and the Akron Wool and Felt Co. He ran an experimental farm and animal husbandry complex, the O.C. Barber Piggery. His first and main endeavor, though, was the manufacture of matches.

One of Barber Match Company's key innovations was in the shape of the matchsticks themselves. Barber's partner obtained United States patent #105,727 in 1870 for "the construction of match-sticks so that said matches shall have thin edges, whereby they more readily ignite…" Using diagonal cuts to carve splints out of solid wood blocks, rather than the conventional horizontal and vertical cuts, increased production efficiency and produced a better splint with sharply angled edges that more readily took a flame. The splints had a distinctive appearance. The cross-section of each matchstick was no longer square, but diamond-shaped, and gave rise to what was undoubtedly the match's most valuable attribute—a catchy name that invoked quality of the highest order. Barber branded the new items as Diamond Matches.

The seeds of the Diamond Match Company's monopoly business—one that caught the attention of Senator Sherman—, had been planted.

War, Taxes and the Birth of Diamond Match

O.C. Barber was born in 1841, and like so many Americans of his generation, his life was shaped in significant ways by the Civil War. Though a fervent supporter of the Union cause, Barber—20 years old at the outbreak of the war—chose to remain in a senior management role at the Barber Match Company rather than join the fight in the trenches. From comments he made later in life, he regretted never having served as a soldier, but perhaps he justified his decision with the notion he was serving in other ways.

Matches were part of the war effort, both operationally and financially. Union soldiers were given strike-anywhere matches as part of their routine supplies, for cooking, warmth, lighting and cannon fire. Matches also helped fund the war effort in the North. In 1862, the federal government imposed a tax on a wide variety of consumer goods and services, from pianos to playing cards. Matches, which by this time had become an everyday household item, were among the items taxed. Manufacturers were required to affix a revenue stamp to each box to indicate the tax had been paid.

The tax was a complicated affair. The stamps had to be printed in some official, certifiable way, and mechanisms were needed —both in companies and in government bureaucracies—to keep track of how much tax was owed, to account for who paid what, and to exercise oversight over the entire process. Although the end tax was the same for all match manufacturers—a penny tax on a box of 100 matches, doubling the price paid by consumers—the impact of the revenue stamp program did not affect small and large manufacturers equally. Procedures, machinery and labor had to be dedicated to affixing the stamps to boxes. The boxes themselves sometimes required modification in order to accept the stamp.

Small firms had to pay the face value of the stamps without delay, while larger firms were offered two significant advantages. Firms that could afford to do so received a discount for buying stamps in bulk from a government-approved printer and were allowed to delay payment if they posted a security bond. An even larger discount was available to those companies that bought their own printing equipment and became approved themselves to print their own stamps—an option open to all in principle, but affordable only to the larger firms.

Although the revenue stamps were widely disliked by both the industry and the public, the larger match manufacturers soon realized the stamps provided them a significant advantage. Access to discounted revenue stamps gave them a competitive edge, and by becoming certified printers, the stamps essentially became a form of advertising. Instead of generic revenue text and a picture of George Washington, the stamps generally featured the company name and an image of the company president.

The unexpected economic advantages of the stamps helped propel the industry on the path to consolidation, with larger companies like Barber Match out-competing their smaller challengers. Adding to that momentum, the revenue stamps also provided the impetus for the industry to come together to discuss their concerns as well as their mutual interests. The first meeting of the Friction Match Makers Association was held in New York City in 1864 (Barber Match did not attend). The group's purpose was quite transparent. It wanted to make changes to the tax system that would be advantageous to the association's members, and, just as importantly, make sure all manufacturers were paying their full share of the tax burden. The Association's charter described its purpose as:

> …consultation and discussion in regard to the best interests of the business, and to determine whether any alterations to the present tax law be

> necessary…also to see what action may be necessary to prevent the many and various modes now resorted to, to evade the present law.

In other words, FMMA wasn't looking for a way to lower their tax burden so much as to ensure that all manufacturers were paying their fair share into the tax system.

The new association was an effective advocate. Its first major victory was obtaining a ruling from the Commissioner of Revenue that imported matches were subject to the same stamp provisions as were domestic suppliers, thereby closing a tax loophole that had provided importers a considerable advantage. All matches sold in the U.S. would now be required to carry the revenue stamp. The group became so comfortable with revenue stamps that it advocated for keeping the tax in place long after the Civil War had ended.

One other issue occupied the match makers as much, if not more, than the revenue stamps. The issue was competition. In particular, the members bemoaned the effect that competition had on the overall match making business. Constant price cutting among manufacturers not only meant minimal profits but, the companies argued, required them to pay substandard wages, forego capital upgrades, and create duplicative networks for transportation and distribution. The effect, in the eyes of the manufacturers, was contrary to the public welfare. In 1879, Barber Match, by now a sizable part of the overall industry, met with other companies to form a new group, the American Match Manufacturers Association, with the express purpose of minimizing competitive pressures. AMMA's primary strategy was price-fixing. Each member agreed to bylaws that included a commitment to set market prices in a fashion that would today be considered blatant market collusion but at the time, was merely considered sensible business practice.

The AMMA members also agreed to:

> …honorably sustain the prices [with]…no deviations, concessions, drawbacks, rebates, discounts, commissions, or variations whatever, under any pretext whatever from the established prices…

Fairly elaborate mechanisms were agreed to, including fines to members and ostracism of distributors, to try and prevent any undermining of the prices. They were to no avail. The agreements collapsed, prices fell again under competitive pressures, and in fairly short order the newfound association was disbanded. Competition grew so fierce that Barber Match, historically a profitable company, began experiencing heavy losses from a price war with its largest competitor, the Swift & Courtney & Beecher Match Company.

The inability to arrange prices through mutual agreements, however frustrating, seemed to launch O.C. Barber in another direction. Rather than attempting to coordinate the activities of a few dozen match manufacturers across the country, Barber set out on a bold, new tactic. He would consolidate the industry as a single corporation, merging with other manufacturers when he could and buying companies outright when he couldn't. The leadership of Swift & Courtney & Beecher agreed to Barber's suggestion for a merger. Other manufacturers quickly followed suit. All told, twelve sizable manufacturers agreed to combine their resources—production operations, distribution channels, intellectual property, process know-how—into a single corporation that took its name from Barber's distinctive brand of product, the Diamond Match Company, incorporated in December 1880 with William Swift as its first president and O.C. Barber as its vice-president.

Diamond Match, flush with cash from the sale of preferred stock, went on an immediate buying spree. The largest matchmaker not yet part of the Diamond enterprise was the Clark Star Match Company, a modern, 400-worker factory in Wisconsin, which Diamond purchased at a substantial premium. The pattern was to be repeated time and again, for facilities large or small, modern or decrepit. Diamond was intent on owning America's match-making capacity, so much so that unprofitable factories were simply purchased and closed. All told, Diamond merged with or bought up thirty-one manufacturers, keeping thirteen of them active and shuttering the rest. Diamond's expenses were substantial, but its strategy of industry consolidation also led to efficiencies of operations. Where five companies had maintained five outlet stores to distribute matches in the city of Chicago, now only one was needed.

All purchases carried an important stipulation: that the previous owners would not re-enter the match business in any fashion for at least a decade, and sometimes longer. An 1887 case, Diamond Match v. Roeber, upheld a contractual obligation for Roeber to avoid all match manufacturing for the next 99 years after the purchase of his match company; a very early example of non-compete clauses that have become so commonplace in modern contracts.

Diamond's expenses were substantial, but its strategy of industry consolidation also led to efficiencies of operations. Barber was committed to running his factories as state-of-the-art facilities. Where five companies had maintained five outlet stores to distribute matches in the city of Chicago, now only one was needed. From an industry-wide perspective, total costs of transportation, storage, sales staff, marketing, and accounting were all reduced. Barber's goals were nothing if not ambitious, as he proudly told shareholders: "The Diamond Match Company has aimed to place its matches in every nook and corner of the United States, at so low a cost to the consumer that he may have no cause for complaint."

For a time, Diamond's consolidation of the industry went largely unnoticed. Only one publication catering to retail outlets, the New York Grocers' Journal, reported on Diamond's early efforts. A January 1881 article, "Monopolising Match Making" concluded that "the new company can do what it pleases so far as fixing prices is concerned. It need fear no competition…" Company histories differ as to the percentage of the American match business that ended up in Diamond's possession, but agree that it was at least 85 percent and perhaps as high as 95 percent in the company's heyday at the turn of the century. One of the small surviving match manufactures advertised their product in 1885 with the slogan "anti-monopoly matches."

International Expansion

As a newly-formed company, Diamond Match quickly made its first international acquisition, buying a match factory in Canada in January 1881. Barber was particularly interested in expanding overseas, but it was not until 1888 that he was able to free himself from domestic responsibilities long enough to take a six-week tour of Europe. He marveled at his experience but was thoroughly appalled at the state of industrialization, working conditions and overall level of poverty he came across, impressions that were reinforced on his return trip in 1894.

Workers' wages were much lower in Europe than in the United States, so much so that Barber noted men and women pulling heavy loads that, in the U.S., would be pulled by horses, a difference he attributed to economics: the upkeep of a horse was more expensive in Europe than the wages of several laborers. Similarly, British factories distributed cardboard to poor households so that matchboxes could be folded and assembled by hand, a process that had long since been accomplished by machinery at Diamond's factories. "May human life never be so cheap in America," Barber told his colleagues back home.

Barber was also surprised by the state of European technology, which he deemed to be about 25 years behind the machinery back home. Perhaps, he pondered, the low price of labor robbed the Europeans of any incentive to modernize their processes. A U.S. style factory in England—combining American know-how with Europe's low wages—would, Barber thought, prove to be an unbeatable combination. Establishing manufacturing operations in England would be far preferable to importing product from the United States. Europe's cheap labor and subsidized merchant marine fleet allowed them to export matches to America, but Barber had neither of these advantages available to him in the reverse direction. European nations also tended towards complex import regulations and substantial tariffs that made import schemes even less desirable.

Interestingly, Barber's European trips reinforced an orientation that was already firmly present in him: Barber, the American capitalist par excellence, did not approve of free trade. He saw the impact of free trade as an unrestrained race to the bottom, forcing firms to cut wages to the lowest levels and scrimp on product quality in order to compete in an undiscriminating market. Continuing his observations of Bryant and May, Barber wrote:

> …Besides their London shops, this firm has several Swedish shops where they pay still less wages and make poorer matches, which is the brand that they shove into [the US] market and to meet it we make a sulphur match that we have to sell to the wholesalers for 35 cents for 14,400 matches… we would have to cut our labor down to meet even the lowest Swedish labor or we would have to shut up our shops entirely…and buy our stock abroad to supply our trade…

Barber returned to Diamond Match to sell the board of directors on his expansion ideas. He had a two-fold plan for international expansion. First, buy a match making company in England to establish an overseas base of operations. Secondly, approach nationalized match-making industries in France, Belgium and other countries with an offer to lease their factories the modernized equipment that Diamond Match had pioneered. Barber felt the machine-leasing opportunities might one day become "the better part of our business." The board agreed, and by 1895, Diamond had purchased its first European company, a small match manufacturer intended as a foothold in England, and as a prelude to building their own state-of-the-art factory, intended to technologically superior and more cost efficient than his English competitors. Barber planned to proceed as his company had in the US: buy up the competing firms until Diamond held a near monopoly in Britain.

Diamond secured patents in more than a dozen European countries as well as in Canada, Mexico, Brazil, India and Australia. They marketed their advanced machinery throughout Europe and to China, Japan and South America. Their international expansion plans involved far more than their foothold in the U.K. After Diamond Ltd was formed in Liverpool in 1897, it was followed swiftly by Diamond of Switzerland, Diamond Match of Russia, and the Diamond Match Company of Germany. Under different names, Diamond also had manufacturing operations in Canada, Brazil, Peru, Chile, the Philippines and South Africa, and machine-leasing arrangements with match manufacturers in Japan. It wasn't long before the expansion companies themselves began to expand, building new operations to extend their marketing areas. In a 1901 interview, Barber remarked: "… We are not making an effort to consolidate the match business of the world, but it is gradually falling into the hands of the Diamond Match Company."

Interestingly, one factor in Diamond's successful venture in England—and eventually, in all its operations—revolved around the first major occupational safety and health issue to receive international attention. A key ingredient in early match-making, white phosphorous, caused a disease among match workers known formally as necrosis of the jaw, and informally as phossy jaw. The disease was, at best, terribly disfiguring and was often fatal. Industry attempts at improved factory hygiene, ventilation and safer handling were only partly successful at avoiding new cases of phossy jaw.

Match workers went on strike in England, in part, to insist on better safety measures in the industry. The situation grew so grim and so notorious that, one by one, countries began limiting the use of white phosphorous, either by banning it outright or taxing it at a rate that made it uneconomical to use. The 1906 Berne Convention, the first international treaty to ban a dangerous chemical, ended the use of white phosphorous in Europe, followed six years later by an American law to do the same.

Diamond had already tried making and selling matches that did not use white phosphorous, but abandoned their initial effort due to consumer preferences for the original matches. However, Diamond's experience, along with patents and licenses it held for alternative match-making processes, left it ideally suited to adroitly switch away from using white phosphorous when so required. Diamond's competitors were not only less capable, but were actually prevented from making the switch without licensing the newer process from Diamond. Although Diamond agreed to make the license available industry-wide without profiting from it (a step that led Scientific American magazine to describe Diamond as a "public benefactor"), Diamond's expertise in this area gave it a considerable advantage over its competitors.

Intrigue

We will briefly mention two episodes in Diamond's history that almost scuttled their international ambitions, but our brevity shouldn't be mistaken for lack of significance, as both events threatened not only expansion but the very capacity of Diamond to continue as a going concern.

The first involved a five-year battle, from 1894 to 1899, with Edwin Gould, son of the well-known railroad magnate Jay Gould. Edwin Gould was determined to enter the match business and founded the Continental Match Company in 1894 for just that purpose. Although Continental appeared to be in head to head competition with Diamond, Gould's actual game plan may well have been otherwise, angling to force Diamond into buying him out (Diamond had already paid premium prices for several other companies) or seeking to merge with Diamond and ultimately take control of the company himself.

Barber might have been able to ignore Continental in other circumstances, but Gould's fierce tactics and deep pockets made the new company a formidable adversary. When Gould found his product locked out of the wholesale distribution chain, he bought up Diamond matches in warehouse quantities and offered them to wholesalers at heavily discounted prices…as long as they would begin distributing Continental matches as well. Gould relentlessly went after Diamond's reputation—and stock price—as part of his overall strategy. When Diamond announced machinery contracts with the French government as *a fait accompli*, Gould's agents in Europe revealed that the contracts were not finalized. In fact, although the contracts had received favorable attention from a mid-level bureaucrat in the appropriate ministry, the senior minister was inclined to back away from Diamond's offer.

Gould fanned the flames of uncertainty, working journalists and financiers with equal success. The stock price of Diamond Match took a severe hit from the negative publicity that Gould engineered, and Gould, as it turned out, was right about France's refusal to finalize the deal. Gould took advantage of his manipulations, shorting Diamond stock when he knew bad news (partly of his own making) was coming. Major shareholders of Diamond were wooed in person, by both Gould and Barber, in an effort to, respectively, undermine or support the stock price. In time, Gould acquired substantial holdings in Diamond and shifted his strategy from manipulating the stock price to managing the company. As his holdings increased, he sent representatives to annual meetings who today would be labelled activist shareholders, demanding information, offering resolutions, insisting on votes and supporting their own slate for the board of directors.

The second episode intertwined in odd ways with the first and with the national politics of the day. While Gould conspired to drive down the price of Diamond stock, company insiders were anticipating just the opposite, that the company's expansion into Europe would excite investors to the point that Diamond stock would double and perhaps redouble in value. After all, the company would then control the lion's share of match production in both the U.S. and Britain and, thorough machinery contracts, have a large piece of the rest of Europe's match industry as well. Anticipating this news, two members of Diamond's board began quietly buying up shares on margin, pooling money from other investors and even using the company's funds as their collateral.

At first, the plan worked handsomely. Diamond made public news of imminent machinery contracts with France (which Gould later refuted), along with its plans for production in England, with immediate effect. The stock rose rapidly, doubling in price in short order. Touting the advantages of its machines and processes, Diamond hosted elaborate tours of its flagship Ohio facility, impressing both European and American businessmen and potential investors. Barber himself led some of the tours, telling reporters:

> It is only a matter of time until the Diamond Company by reason of its superior progress will make matches for the world. No country can

> compete with us at this time. With our machinery we save fully 75 percent on labor over any other process in use anywhere.

Several monkey wrenches were thrown into the stock scheme. One of these was William Jennings Bryan, whose political ascendancy in the election of 1896 frightened the investing community. Bryan advocated abandoning the gold standard as the basis of America's currency, a position seen as financially dangerous both domestically and in Europe. Investors, only recently recovered from the Panic of 1893, grew more hesitant, especially with speculative investments like the growth in Diamond share price. Barber himself predicted that, were Bryan to be elected, "…the greatest financial crisis this country ever saw, will follow."

At the same time, Edwin Gould, continuing his campaign to drive down his competitor's stock price, unearthed the aforementioned powerful piece of information that Barber had not secured a contract with the French government, despite Diamond's announcement to the contrary. On top of all else, a large fire destroyed a significant portion of Diamond's standing stock of lumber. The combination of events was enough to spook the financiers who had extended credit for the purchase of Diamond stock. When they insisted on a margin call, the two Diamond board members were unable to come up with the cash. When the French deal collapsed, a lot of Diamond's credibility went with it and failure of several board members to pay their margin debt just made matters worse.

News of the failure led to consternation and rumors. *Is the stock price inflated? Were investors misled about Europe? Was Diamond going bankrupt?* For a few days in August 1896 financial markets trembled. The Chicago Stock Exchange, where the margin trading had been carried out, was forced to close for an extended period to avoid panic selling. Gould pounded Diamond's credibility in public statements, letters to the editor, privately to investors, and at every other opportunity. Diamond used the same methods in its attempt to reassure the world that the company was solvent and doing well.

Eventually, the storm passed, helped, in no small measure, by the intervention of Chicago financiers, George Pullman and Phillip Armour. The errant board members were roundly scolded and Diamond's bylaws were amended to prevent such surreptitious use of company funds in the future. But Gould continued to chip away at the company's reputation, all the while continuing to amass Diamond stock. By 1898, Gould was Diamond's largest shareholder. O.C. Barber requested a meeting and, salesman that he was, convinced his adversary that Gould's best interests would be served by abandoning Continental Match (which had been unprofitable) and taking steps to improve rather than disparage Diamond's market status. With Barber's backing, Gould himself would be guaranteed a place on the board.

The deal was done. Gould joined Diamond's board in 1899 at the same time that Diamond purchased Continental Match. The two companies were now one, and Barber and Gould were no longer corporate adversaries. Diamond's strategy did not appear to change, as the company remained intent on buying up as much competing match manufacturing capacity as possible, along with the underlying intellectual property that continued to drive innovations in the industry. Once again, Barber's brand of anti-competitive capitalism came to the fore. "The object," he wrote, "is primarily to terminate the cut-throat competition which has been impairing the profits for several years…"

Waning Years

O.C. Barber remained at the helm of Diamond until 1909, retiring when he was 68 years old. Diamond's dominance of the global match industry seemed to pass with him as several factors conspired to lessen the company's presence.

In some respects, the company was a victim of its own success. Diamond built its business on boxed, wooden matches. It did not invent paper matches in the now-familiar matchbook, but Diamond put them into marketable and usable form.

Two innovations in particular—moving the striking surface from the inside of the matchbook to the outer surface, and adding the simple message: "Close cover before striking"—transformed the matchbook from a cumbersome, dangerous and unpopular item to one that was safe and simple. Diamond's first major order for their user-friendly book matches came from the Pabst Brewing Company, which ordered ten million books and took advantage of yet another innovation, in marketing this time, by printing the Pabst logo on the cover. Book matches were cheap enough that companies like Pabst could hand them out for free. Too cheap, in fact. With paper matches freely available, prices for wooden matches fell, even as raw material costs were on the rise, depressing profit margins in the industry.

A newfound competitor, the Ohio Match Company, appeared in 1895 and was quickly sued for patent infringement, Diamond arguing that its competitor's machinery was too close in design to Diamond's patented processes. The courts did not agree, however. Ohio Match's successful defense of its technologies provided it with staying power in the industry and marked the end of Diamond's strategy of buying up all its competitors. Foreign competition resurfaced as well, having learned to take advantage of both newer technologies and cheaper labor. These firms not only challenged Diamond in other countries, but also at home through aggressive and low-priced imports.

Technological changes beyond the match industry itself also took a toll. Inventions ranging from electric lights to cigarette lighters were relegating matches to 'last century's' technology, no longer the essential household item used by everyone, every day. Relying on matches as a major source of income was becoming an increasingly less viable business model. Diamond survives to this day as the major manufacturer of wooden matches in the United States (though no longer the international powerhouse of old) but has diversified, under the name Diamond Brands, into a range of other household products, from plastic cutlery to wooden clothespins. Operating as a subsidiary of the Jarden Corporation, Diamond Brands competes against hundreds of other manufacturers around the world that manufacture similar household items, and appears to rely on consumer recognition of its well-known brand name as a key asset to distinguish its products from the competition.

Was Diamond Match an Early Amazon?

The story of Diamond Match is interesting in its own right, but we present it here as something of a foundational tale. In making the transition from a mom and pop (*well...just pop*) operation hand-dipping matches in a small barn, to a near-monopoly dominating the global match making industry, we can see the emergence of the modern multinational corporation. Diamond Match had features very similar to the giant firms of today, whether in the United States, Europe, Japan or the not-quite capitalistic economies of China, Russia and much of the Middle East.

The story of Diamond Match is also the story of Apple, Tesla Motors, Volkswagen, Virgin Atlantic, Electrolux, Saudi Aramco and thousands of other firms with less familiar names. Like Coca-Cola, hoping to be the drink of choice for consumers all over the world, Diamond Match truly embraced the global marketplace like few companies before it. While each company history is unique, each company has to grapple, as Diamond did, with the entangled complexities of finance, politics, public opinion, regulation and technology that characterize modern business.

It goes without saying that the world in the early decades of the 21st century is very different from Diamond's world of 100-125 years ago. For one thing, the nearly complete monopoly position Diamond was able to achieve not just in U.S., but in global match manufacturing, would not be tolerated in the modern era. O.C. Barber's open disdain for competition and active embrace of price-fixing would not happen nearly as publicly in the modern age, (though the sentiments and practices can certainly still be found). But neither are the differences between Barber's world and our own so profound as to make Diamond's business environment unrecognizable.

Comparing an industrial giant of old with a dominant company in the present day reveals the similarities and some of the differences between then and now. We have chosen Amazon for the comparison. Both companies were founded by men with a singular and fiercely competitive vision, committed to not only utilizing the technologies of their day, but responding nimbly to changes in technology and markets, and fostering change itself when it suited the companies' purposes.

Barber recognized the enormous competitive advantage that 19th-century "high tech" provided; electric lights were no less remarkable in Barber's day than self-driving cars are today. Barber knew he could best maintain that advantage by pushing the technology forward with new advances and by aggressively taking ownership of the intellectual property behind those advances.

So too with Amazon. If anything, Amazon's founder and CEO, Jeff Bezos, is even more committed to technology than was O.C. Barber. Amazon has embraced technological sophistication in a manner that far surpasses any other online retailer. Diamond Match and Amazon both relied on technology not only for operational efficiencies but as a central part of their business model; Diamond leased its state-of-the-art equipment to other companies worldwide and Amazon's web services company rents space in "the cloud" that is used by other online companies like Netflix and Samsung.

Barber and Bezos both went on extensive acquisition sprees. Barber focused on buying up the nation's (and to an extent, the world's) match manufacturing capacity, and also started numerous other companies with far-flung ventures ranging from railroads to pig farms. Bezos, thus far, keeps most acquisitions under the Amazon umbrella, even scooping up the Whole Foods supermarket chain, but operates separate businesses as well including the Washington Post and the space tourism company, Blue Origin.

It was not just machinery that gave Diamond an edge. Like its modern-day counterparts, Diamond used its portfolio of patents for machinery and for the chemistry of match-making to great effect. Diamond's intellectual property gave the company enormous leverage in preventing other firms from adopting the best technologies available. Amazon's intellectual property holdings make it one of the world's technology leaders. It holds more than 7,000 US patents as compared with about 1,400 for eBay and 350 for Walmart. The giant Chinese online retailer, Alibaba, holds about 400 US patents although its international patent portfolio is significantly larger. Amazon spends more on R&D than any other company in the world.

The companies' deep pockets didn't hurt either, when it came to dealing with patent issues. Multiple patent cases, with Diamond as both plaintiff and defendant, have a modern ring to them, as the courts tried to work out the details of a particular technology and the degree to which one piece of machinery or one chemical process resembles or differs from another. Diamond Match and Union Match got into an extended legal scuffle over Diamond's 1895 patent for a machine to fill match boxes (US538535). Diamond's claim of infringement was initially upheld by the court but subsequently overturned by an appellate court in 1908. Though Diamond lost this particular case, few companies had the resources to engage in a decade-long battle over intellectual property rights.

Amazon is also involved in extensive and long-term litigation over patents. The company spent a decade and untold millions of dollars defending its patent for Amazon's "one click" shopping cart system prior to the patent's expiration in 2017. The defense was money well-spent as Amazon was able to license one-click to other retailers, including Apple which used it for its iTunes store.

Diamond was also one of the first companies to reach the world-wide consumer market. The company was truly the match maker to the world. Technology played a role here as well. In a restraint-of-trade case from 1887, Diamond Match v Roeber, the justices noted: "Steam and electricity have, for the purposes of trade and commerce, almost annihilated distance, and the whole world is now a mart for the distribution of the products of industry." The whole world, indeed: Diamond was as familiar to households in its day as Amazon is today.

Although its focus outside the United States was largely on the wealthy markets of Europe, the Diamond Match Company was well-positioned to supply matches to India, China, Japan, Australia, Africa and South America. In regions where it didn't supply matches directly, it provided much of the machinery that made match manufacturing viable. Diamond's global reach is very reminiscent of how companies do business in the modern era. Amazon's goal is to be nothing less than "Earth's most customer-centric Company". About a third of their sales and operations are outside of North America; Amazon's website in India is the most-visited site in the country.

Products are routinely marketed across broad swathes of the globe these days, a practice that Diamond, as much as any other firm, can be said to have pioneered. British match manufacturers like Bryant and May appealed to consumers' national sense of pride to help compete against the 'foreign' competition of Diamond Match. The strategy was successful for a while, but was not enough to forestall Diamond's dominance in the industry.

Less familiar in today's world is a common consumer product so completely dominated by a single enterprise. Coke has Pepsi to compete against it, McDonalds has Burger King and KFC. But Diamond stood almost alone in the match market. Even Nike, the most dominant brand of athletic footwear, has approximately 50 percent of the U.S. market and around 30% of the world market. Only a few technology companies—Google in the search market, Intel in computer chips—have achieved a level of market dominance that approach the level of Diamond's dominance in its heyday. Amazon dominates in a few categories—it is far and away the largest seller of ebooks, for example—but dominates more by the diversity and scale of its operations than by cornering any particular market for consumer goods.

Diamond also diversified its operations in a very modern fashion. Barber's father made matches in his backyard "factory" buying or making his mixing vats, cutting tools, chemicals and wood blocks on an ad hoc basis. O.C. Barber made matches as well, but the global reach of Diamond's activities meant the company handled materials on a scale so large that it almost naturally extended into other lines of business. Diamond's need for sources of wood near to its facilities turned the company into a large landholder, especially of forest land, and an owner of large lumber milling operations. These were initially close to the company's Ohio roots but eventually, Diamond managed extensive land holdings across the U.S., in Canada and at its overseas operations. Lumber that was unsuited for match-making was sold for other purposes; Diamond's western forest land holdings were one of the key suppliers of wood for the west coast building boom in the decades that followed the California Gold Rush as well as a major source of lumber for the rebuilding of San Francisco after the 1906 earthquake.

Barber owned a furniture company, a pipe manufacturer, a fire sprinkler firm and numerous other enterprises. Diamond Match didn't buy very much match-making machinery. It made its own in the company's state-of-the-art machine shops and did almost as much business renting machinery as it did selling matches. Diamond built two complete company towns: Barberton, Ohio and Barber, California, building and running its own railroad in the latter.

Ultimately, Diamond was forced into a strategy of product diversity by weaknesses in its historical business of match-making. Its diversification was a sign of its weakening dominance. For Amazon, the situation, for the time being at least, is much the reverse. The corporation's aggressive diversification beyond its original focus on selling books has established Amazon as the leading retailer of the internet age.

Perhaps it is Diamond's corporate history (and Barber's personal history) as a shaper of—and being shaped by—public policy that is most familiar in the modern age. The Diamond Match Company found itself facing a need to respond almost continually to political influence and societal concerns. The company's roots were enmeshed in the enormous upheaval of the Civil War, and Diamond came of age during America's so-called Progressive Age—an era when rapid communications, mistrust of corporations, labor strife and muckraking journalism blended together in a particularly modern fashion. The most visible aspect of this was Diamond's reaction to public alarm over the occupational disease, phossy jaw, an issue that was covered extensively in newspapers and magazines, highlighted in Congressional floor speeches, addressed in Europe through an international treaty, and finally made the subject of a thorough U.S. government investigation that painted a damming picture of the state of affairs in the U.S. match industry.

Diamond's response ran a gamut entirely familiar to a modern audience, from initial silence on the issue, to denying that phossy jaw was a problem—at least not at Diamond's state of the art facilities—to eventually agreeing, at the direct urging of the President of the United States, that something needed be done (one is reminded of President Trump tweeting missives aimed at influencing individual companies, whether to lower the cost of Air Force One, change their news programming, or keep a factory in the United States). The company's seemingly magnanimous gesture of making its safety match patent available to all, at no cost, actually solved a complex political bottleneck that threatened to scuttle legislative action that Diamond hoped to see move forward.

Amazon has also made magnanimous gestures, especially its 2018 announcement that it is raising the minimum amount it pays its quarter of a million U.S. workers to $15 an hour, about twice the federal minimum wage. The raise, as reported in the NY Times, amounted to an acknowledgement that the company was "feeling squeezed by political pressure". The company's involvement in policy issues covers a broad spectrum, ranging from advocating for a raise in the federal minimum wage to keeping airspace available for commercial drone use. Politics played a role in the company's decision to build new "second headquarters" operations in both Alexandria, Virginia and New York City, and was instrumental, as well, in Amazon's eventual announcement to scuttle its NYC plans. Amazon has also made a substantial commitment to environmental and social sustainability, a topic we will return to in Chapter 8.

Diamond Match and Amazon both heralded the arrival of business operations that were simply different than any the world had previously experienced. The differences were not totally a matter of new technologies. But technology was certainly at the heart of much of the innovations made by both companies.

CHAPTER 6

CORPORATIONS AND PATENTS

Diamond Match's and Amazon's focus on their patent portfolios is hardly unusual. Corporations as well as individual inventors fought over patent rights for almost every major invention in modern history and an awful lot of less significant inventions as well. Eli Whitney's company manufacturing the cotton gin went bankrupt from the cost of patent infringement lawsuits. Cyrus McCormick, founder of what would eventually become International Harvester, spent decades fighting patent battles over the mechanical reaper. Thomas Edison, perhaps the most prolific patent-holder ever, was forced to bring in a competitor as a corporate partner to market the lightbulb after Edison lost an important patent lawsuit. He was so active in patent litigation that he has been dubbed a "patent troll" by some modern historians (more about patent trolls in a while). So, too, with the Wright Brothers, whose extended patent battles consumed the latter part of their lives and are generally thought to have set back advancements in American aviation by more than a decade.

Samuel Colt's fondness for patents was built right into his company name: the Patent Arms Manufacturing Company. Samuel Morse's 1840 patent for the telegraph was contested all the way to the Supreme Court, which ruled only partly in Morse's favor in the landmark 1853 decision, O'Reilly v Morse. Polaroid sued Kodak over instant photography. Everyone sues everyone over cell phones: Apple and Samsung have filed more than a dozen lawsuits against each other in what has come to be known as the smartphone patent wars.

Patent litigation, from all appearances, has accelerated in the modern era. Long-term data on the number of infringement lawsuits is scattered and difficult to interpret, but the size of patent awards has mushroomed in recent decades. The creation in the US of a special patent court in the 1980s provided judicial expertise and a streamlined, more predictable process for pursuing infringement cases. Infringement awards skyrocketed;

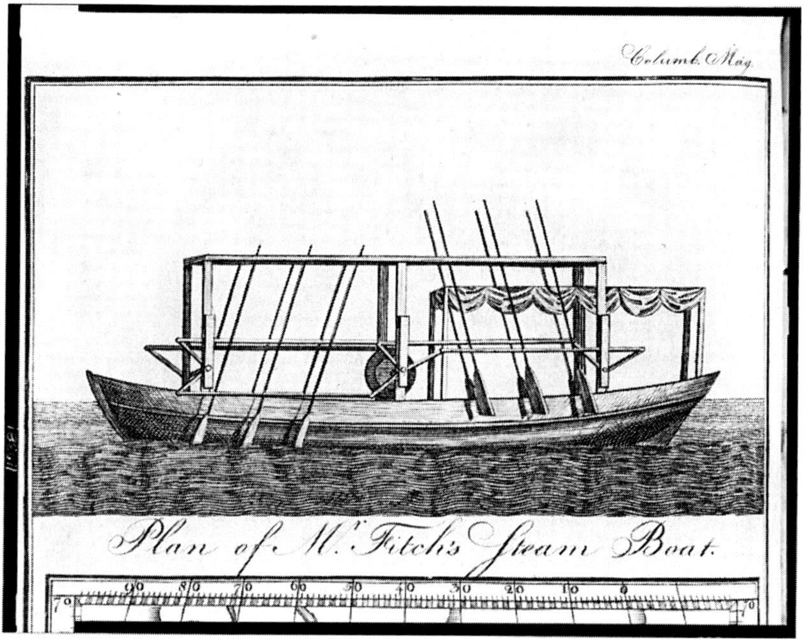

Figure 6-1: One of the earliest functional steamboats

where settlements of more than a few million dollars had been relatively uncommon, awards grew quickly into billion-dollar-plus amounts.

An online search of *billion dollar patent lawsuit* highlights dozens of giant companies suing one another, or engaged in litigation against less well-known but equally truculent foes. Litigation in the communications and medical arenas is particularly robust. A few example headlines:

- Samsung facing $3 billion dollar lawsuit over patent infringement
- Patent troll VirnetX granted half a billion dollar verdict against Apple
- Apple paid Nokia $2 billion as part of a patent lawsuit settlement
- Anatomy of a billion dollar patent drug dispute - the Merck Keytruda patent
- Medtronic To Pay Over $1Billion To Settle Patent Litigation With Edwards Lifesciences
- Microsoft Vs Samsung in a billion dollar patent dispute
- Google-Oracle lawsuit revived—billions on the line

- Caltech wins a $1.1-billion patent verdict against Apple and Broadcom

And there are many more to choose from, of course.

Patents aren't only a means of business protection. They are a business in their own right. IBM's portfolio of more than 40,000 U.S. patents is worth many billions of dollars, and the company earns more than $1 billion a year licensing its technologies. Google bought Motorola for $12.5 billion, largely to acquire the latter's patents.

Thomas Kuhn's early essay, The Essential Tension, highlights the tug of war that exists between a desire for innovation and a reluctance to move away from the status quo of accepted practice and knowledge. Although Kuhn's frame of reference was the process of basic science, the same might be said for technological invention. Patent holders have their own form of essential tension: the desire to invent, refine, improve and leapfrog new technologies while simultaneously inhibiting others from doing so. The patent system reinforces the tension of industrial innovation in highly competitive markets, whether match-making *a la* Diamond Match, or match-making *a la* dating (Match.com, owner of Tinder and other dating services, is embroiled in several patent infringement lawsuits).

There was a time in history when corporations and patents were not clearly distinct concepts. Early corporations were granted by a patent process, much as land patents were used (and to some extent, still are) as a grant of property. Patents, like corporations, evolved from an infrequently-offered privilege to something akin to a fundamental right. This chapter takes a bit of a side excursion to explore the interesting intersection between patents and corporations.

What Did Inventors Want from Patents? ...a Quick History

A patent is a government offer of permission, protection and encouragement. But permission to do what, protection from what, and encouragement in what form are matters that have varied enormously during the history of patents.

The term patent is shorthand for the original phrase *letters patent*, a reference to a letter issued by a government authority, typically a monarch or legislature. The letters were 'patent' in the same sense we speak of something as patently obvious...apparent, open, available for anyone to see. *Letters close*, in contrast, were eyes-only documents intended for a single recipient; letters close were typically folded and secured with an official wax seal. Letters patent were issued as open sheets for general consumption, carrying a seal that identified the importance of the document, but didn't actually seal it.

Official patents could be (and were) issued for just about anything. Letters patent included promises of funding, grants of territory, exclusive access to markets, incorporations of a town or business, permission to import or export, citizenship, pardons for crimes, and rights to accept apprentices, launch an expedition, host a fair, and establish a coat of arms. Blackstone's 1769 description captures their essence:

> The king's grants are also a matter of public record... These grants, whether of lands, honours, liberties, franchises or ought besides are contained in charters, or letters patent that is, open letters...

Note that Blackstone equates letters patents to charters. Corporate charters and inventor patents, as these terms are currently understood, have their legalistic roots in the same system of letters patent

The subject matter of letters patent was so broad that, even at the relatively late date of Blackstone's discussion of letters patent, the topic of patents specifically for inventions is not even mentioned. However, a substantial subset of patents focused on commercial activities and a small subset of these were invention patents, granting specific rights for innovations. The Patent Rolls of Henry VI include a patent dated April 3, 1449 to one John Utynam for the creation of stained glass, a document sometimes considered the first invention patent issued in English (a 1444 patent granted to an alchemist to "transmute imperfect metals ...into perfect gold" doesn't quite make the grade).

This early patent took a very broad view of innovation, extending as it did, privileges not only for new ideas but for known ideas that were newly-introduced to Britain. Utynam had not invented any techniques for making stained glass but had learned the art in Flanders and agreed to import his know-how to England. The patent granted Utynam a lifetime salary from the King and a twenty year exclusive period during which only he and his shop could make and sell stained glass. In return, the patent committed Utynam to provide stained glass for several English colleges and to "instruct divers lieges of the King" in stained glass and other arts to which Utynam was privy.

Letters patent, in other words, were official decrees. Queen Elizabeth was particularly fond of issuing letters patent, using them to create, during her reign, as many as 80 areas of commercial privilege—in effect, mini-monopolies—for inventors, importers of skills like Utynam, or to individuals favored by the Crown. Some Elizabethan patents covered true inventions and bear some similarity to the patent system as we know it today. Others, like the patent issued for salt, had nothing to do with invention or innovation and merely existed to create a monopoly, allowing only selected merchants to sell a commodity, typically at exorbitant prices, with commensurate benefits to the royal coffers.

The egregious nature of some letters patent led to a backlash among both commoners and the power elite in England. Edward Darcy, a member of Queen Elizabeth's court, held a monopoly patent for the sale of playing cards and took the (in hindsight, unwise) step of bringing another merchant to court for selling cards without Darcy's permission. The English courts ruled, in 1599, that the original grant of a monopoly was invalid as there was no legal basis for creating a monopoly when the only outcome was for private gain without any broader public good. The decision, known as the Case of Monopolies, was a direct challenge to the authority of the English monarchy. Two decades later, Parliament passed the Statute of Monopolies, effectively nullifying all previously-issued commercial patents and, going forward, restricting new patents to actual inventions, allowing the "true and first inventor" to receive the protection of letters patent for a period of fourteen years. With the passage of the law in 1624, the patent system came into being in a form that begins to look familiar to us today; it would be another 200 years before Britain substantially revised its patent laws.

Early patents were largely a grant of privilege, an option available to the monarch to issue or not issue, letters patent based on whatever policy consideration, personal relationship, or private whim so moved the King or Queen on any given request. The Statue of Monopolies imposed limits on the monarch's patent-granting authority but created no obligation to respond to patent requests. In the United States, the first patent law essentially established patents as a right. An inventor who followed procedure was owed a finding; the law did not guarantee that every patent request would be granted, but it did establish a barebones process by which such requests could be made and how they were to be evaluated and responded to.

Although British patents originated with the monarch in principle, in practice the King or Queen had less and less involvement with patents in the period after the Statute of Monopolies. Instead, a decidedly Byzantine bureaucracy emerged for submitting and finalizing patents that added to the time, cost and complexity of procuring a British patent.

The early British patent system, as one historian noted, "...worked so poorly that during the 150 years following the beginning of the numbering of English patents...scarcely more than 1000 patents were issued..." For example, obstetrical forceps, invented by the Chamberlen family of male midwives in 1598, were not patented due to the absence of a reliable patent system. Instead, the inventors went to enormous lengths to keep their discovery secret. "For over a century, women around the world had died in childbirth because the Chamberlen family had no effective way of profiting from the family invention except by maintaining it as a trade secret."

Patents in the United States

Scarcely a year after the new government of the United States came into being Congress passed the nation's first Patent Act on April 10, 1790. The law appointed a triumvirate of very senior government officials—the Secretaries of the Department of War and the Department of State, along with the Attorney General—to review patent requests and, when merited, grant patents for inventions of significant import.

The high priority the young nation gave to establishing authority and creating a working system for patents looks, at first blush, to be entirely consistent with the type of inventiveness, entrepreneurship and can-do attitude that so characterized the young nation. Post-revolutionary America was in desperate need of building a manufacturing base, as its economy was largely agrarian and its geographic isolation from European markets meant that importing manufactured goods was difficult, uncertain and expensive. Mercantile laws like the British Iron Act of 1750 were designed to stifle manufacturing operations in America, so that the colonies would have to purchase manufactured goods from England. Independence now meant that manufacturing in the United States could begin to thrive in an unfettered fashion.

It's not clear that the young nation's community of inventors were vociferously and unanimously clamoring for patent protection. That many were, there is no doubt. But there were prominent naysayers as well. One of early America's most notable inventors not only never held a patent, but positively saw no good use for them. Benjamin Franklin—whose projects and discoveries included the Franklin stove, the lightning rod, bifocal glasses, musical instruments and even swimming fins—was of the opinion that ideas, even ideas made concrete in the form of inventions, should circulate as freely as possible. Patents did nothing more than stifle this free exchange.

Franklin's contemporary, Thomas Jefferson, had an almost equally-diversified track record of inventions, having created or improved devices for farming, furniture, household implements, ciphers and even an early type of copying machine. But Jefferson, too, was wary of patents, and even disdainful of them as a tool of government. Jefferson correctly saw patents as a government-sanctioned monopoly, albeit a temporary one. As a staunch anti-monopolist, even the limited form of monopoly proposed for the patent system did not sit well with him. Jefferson was dismayed that the draft of the Constitution did not include an outright ban on monopolies.

Jefferson and Franklin may well have been prominent exceptions to the rule however, Colonial governments were familiar with the English system of granting patents to inventors. Colonies often granted patents prior to the founding of the United States by individual acts of the state legislatures. Several of the founding fathers, including James Madison and Noah Webster, were explicit supporters of creating a patent system or, at the least, wrote favorably about the desirability of protecting intellectual property.

The Patent Act of 1790, enacted on April 10 of that year, weighed in at a relatively compact 1,400 words (in comparison, the 1952 Patent Act that lays out the framework of the modern system is about 144,000 words). The new law, subtitled "An Act to promote the progress of useful Arts" can be summarized in a similarly compact manner:

- Any person or group with a "sufficiently useful and important" invention or discovery can petition the government for a patent.
- The petition is reviewed by at least two of three of the following: Secretary of State, Secretary of War and the Attorney General.

- If granted, the patent, formally issued by the President, confers exclusive rights to the invention for a period of up to fourteen years.
- Patents must be sufficiently well-described to allow others "skilled in the art" to recreate the invention once the patent lapses.
- Patents are publicly available.
- Courts can decide if a patent has been infringed, or if a patent is invalid; the law describes penalties as well.
- Fees for patent applications range from ten cents per page of patent application to three dollars for an actual patent grant with the great seal affixed.

European countries already had well-established patent systems of their own and an impressive record of technological invention. But from the outset, obtaining a United States patent was easier, more open and less expensive than it was in other countries. For inventors, it was no longer necessary to seek an audience with the Queen, to inveigle a high-ranking minister for favors, convince the powers-that-be of the benefits to the state for a particular innovation, or negotiate a convoluted and expensive bureaucracy. The request for a patent was not only easier, but available to all citizens. The act is even (surprisingly) gender-neutral; whereas English patents were granted exclusively to men, the first US patent law specifically invites any inventor, be it "he, she, or they" to petition for a patent.

In a wonderfully ironic twist of history, the preeminent anti-patent, anti-monopoly statesman of the time, Thomas Jefferson in his role as President Washington's Secretary of State, was the de facto head of the early patent process. Although he would later come to recognize the value of the patent system, there is no evidence that, in 1790, his views opposing monopolies in any form had softened. Jefferson was also the most mechanically sophisticated of the commissioners and perhaps more prone than the others to examine each application for its unique technical merits.

Despite its innovations, the 1790 law did not open a floodgate of patents in America; only three patents were granted in 1790, 33 in 1791 and 11 in 1792 (it's not known how many patent applications were rejected in these early years). But the patents covered a broad, diverse field of activities. Inventors filed for patent protections for a wide variety of innovations: a new process for making potash for fertilizer; improvements to the printing press; a machine for spinning cotton and another, dubbed the "wheel of knives" for working with cloth.

The new patent law gave the commissioners little guidance as to how to proceed with their first round of patent reviews. What details must inventors provide? Are technical drawings of an invention required? Is a description of an invention adequate, or must it exist in demonstrable, physical form? Would a model be sufficient? Who has priority: the first idea of an invention, the first demonstration of it, or the first to file a patent? Does a patent issued in England have significance in the United States? How broad is a patent grant? How exclusive?

Eventually, these questions, and others, became so troublesome, and the review process so burdensome, that the 1790 patent law was abandoned, and a new law passed in 1793 throwing the baby out with the bathwater. Rather than amend the review process to make it more manageable, the law eliminated review all together and turned patents into a mere pro forma procedure: apply for a patent, pay the fee, and the patent is yours. Congress basically passed along to the courts the thorny problem of deciding which of these patent grants were legitimate and which were not. It was only in 1836 that a patent system beginning to resemble the current one, with expert review by a staff of patent examiners, came into being.

Powering a New Nation: The Steam Age

The most robust area of innovation, the area calling for the most patents, was the steam engine. Steam was to the 18th century what electricity was to the 19th, petroleum to the 20th and computers to the 21st; a broad area of technological innovation that promised to revolutionize the economy and very way of life for the nations and people of each era. The Newcomen steam engine invented around 1712 and James Watt's improvements in 1767 were rapidly augmenting muscle, water and wind power in Britain and finding expanded applications in mining and factories for pumping water and powering machinery. By the late 1780's Britain probably had well over 1,000 working steam engines in use.

America, in contrast, had three: two in New England and a third for pumping water in a copper mine in Passaic, NJ. The three engines had not been manufactured in the United States; no one in America was especially knowledgeable about the details of building steam-powered machinery. They were instead manufactured across the Atlantic and most-likely smuggled out of England in direct defiance of strict laws prohibiting the export of a technology at the heart of Britain's growing industrial might.

Though Americans knew little of the nuts and bolts about steam engines, it's fair to say they were smitten with the idea...the promise...of powering things with steam. In particular, with the country's vast area (almost twenty times the size of England) of mostly roadless wilderness, forest land, mountains and rivers—especially rivers—Americans were taken with the idea of steam-powered boats. Of the first hundred U.S. patents granted between 1790 and 1795, 14 were steam-related patents and another ten were probably steam patents, though the patent title (which is all that remains of the historical record for many early patents) is not definitive. An 1804 Congressional report notes that "After the close of our Revolution, a sort of mania began to prevail...for impelling boats by steam engines."

No fewer than a dozen 18th century inventors and would-be inventors envisioned steamboats of wildly varying design, including John Fitch and James Rumsey, who vied famously (and bitterly) for recognition as operating America's first steamboat. Designs included steam powered paddle boards and paddle wheels, steam powered oars, steam powered poles that pushed against the river bottom and even a boat propelled by "duck feet", panels that open and closed, pushing against the water, powered by steam.

While Rumsey, Fitch and other inventors in the United States were struggling with the technology of steam—first, to make a reliable engine and second, to make a viable business of steamboat transport—Robert Fulton was mastering the technology and securing finances in Europe.

Fulton had no formal training as an engineer but had a prolific aptitude for invention. A Pennsylvanian, he traveled to London in 1786 to pursue his career as a painter. Despite his success in this regard, Fulton became increasingly interested in mechanical and civil engineering projects. He held several English patents in areas as varied as spinning flax and moving boats over land, and published a 1796 pamphlet, *A Treatise on the Improvement of Canal Navigation*. He worked on submarines and torpedoes for the French government, offering to destroy British ships, and did the same for the British, offering to destroy French ships.

During his tenure in France, Fulton made the acquaintance of Robert Livingston, a well-to-do New Yorker from the town of Clermont.

Livingston, a prominent lawyer, was one of the drafters of the Declaration of Independence and swore in George Washington to his first term as President. Thomas Jefferson appointed him the United States ambassador to France, where he negotiated the Louisiana Purchase. Livingston was also deeply interested in steam and steamboats. He had earlier contracted with another steamboat enthusiast and fellow New Yorker, Nicholas Roosevelt, to pursue the design of working steamboat, but the two parted ways after differing on the best path forward. Roosevelt advocated for a paddle-wheel steamboat, a design that Livingston wasn't prepared to accept, even though he and Fulton would eventually build just such a boat (and would work with Roosevelt again in later years).

In Fulton, Livingston found a kindred soul who not only shared his interests but had the technical skills and boat-building experience more agreeable to Livingston. With influence and funds, Livingston helped Fulton build a steamboat in France and arrange a demonstration on the Seine in 1803. The boat sank, but the men were not deterred. Livingston appears to have persuaded Fulton to continue his steamboat work in the U.S. and used his influence in New York to have the legislature revoke an existing monopoly on steamboats held by John Fitch and pass a new law granting the rights to Livingston.

The business relationship between the two men was formalized in Paris in 1802 when Fulton and Livingston agreed to bring their steamboat operations into being in New York. Their agreement is an intriguing confluence of several different historical streams: Livingston's familiarity with New York politics; Fulton's experience with European patents; the existing patent process in the US; and the morphing of the traditional business partnership into an entity beginning to resemble a corporation.

The Livingston-Fulton agreement consisted of seven "conditions" that detailed specifics like the route from New York City to Albany, the size and capacity of the steamboat, Livingston's initial financial contribution (and Fulton's promise to repay it should the steamboat fail), and practical matters such as creating a process to withdraw from the agreement or dealing with the death of a partner. A key condition revolved around the steamboat patent:

> Second: That a patent shall be taken in the United States of America in the name of said Fulton for a new mechanical combination of a boat to navigate by the power of a Steam Engine for which Patent the said Fulton shall deposit every necessary drawing, model, and specification, and when

> such patent is obtained, the property thereof shall be divided into One hundred shares, fifty of which shares shall be transferred to the said Livingston as his property, and fifty shares shall be held by the said Fulton as his property….

The patent, in essence, has become the business, though the two partners added language to their agreement insuring the business would continue even after the patent lapsed when its 14-year term ended.

Fulton and Livingston are looking to establish a steamboat monopoly, one that a patent will provide for a time, but one that may also be available if the inventors can obtain special "privilege" from one or more states. Their initial success in their endeavor would eventually lead to one of the groundbreaking decisions by the Supreme Court regarding business operations in the United States.

In 1803, Fulton ordered a newly-designed steam engine from the British firm of Boulton and Watt, but the sale was held up by the British government, reluctant to ship such valuable technology to an overseas competitor. It was not until 1806 that the government finally granted permission for the export and the engine was shipped to New York, where Livingston and Fulton could get to work. In 1807, the two men launched the *North River Steamboat of Clermont*, in deference to Livingston's home at Clermont Manor. Later known simply as The Clermont, the vessel offered regular service from New York City to Albany and ushered in the age of the steamboat.

The Clermont, along with subsequent steamboats, ran under the auspices of the North River Steam Boat Company. It's not clear to us why Fulton and Livingston did not incorporate their company. Perhaps Livingston's wealth, and his willingness to fund much of the operation, obviated the need for raising huge amounts of funds that the corporate form made possible. Steamboats were not railroads or canals, after all, and did not require enormous investments in infrastructure. Once the finances for the boat were secured, there was only a modest need for additional capital.

It may also be the case that the two entrepreneurs felt they already had what they needed: monopoly protections provided both by the patents held by Fulton and the exclusivity grant obtained from New York by Livingston. In an era where corporate charters and letters patent were not yet entirely distinct, going back to the state legislature for a corporate charter may have seemed an unneeded step.

Whatever the rationale, the absence of corporate status came back to bite the company in numerous law cases that fell to Livingston's heirs to contend with. An 1820 case heard by the NY courts, for example, Livingston v Lynch
pitted the shareholders of the North River Steamboat Company against one another when a minority shareholder disagreed with measures that had been approved and implemented by the majority. At the heart of Livingston v. Lynch was the question of whether or not the North River Steam Boat Company was a corporation:

> ...the defendants applied to the legislature, and obtained an act incorporating the company; but the plaintiff refused to join in the application, or to become a corporator.

In Chapter 1, one of the enumerated characteristics of a corporation was centralized management, the separation of shareholders from a professional team of managers who made the company's major operational decisions. It was exactly this sort of separation that the majority shareholders were seeking, so that the company could be run more nimbly, without requiring unanimous consent of all shareholders for all significant decisions. But the act of incorporating was itself being challenged as a step that was not agreed to by all shareholders. After a lengthy legal battle, the court sided with Lynch, nothing that: "In private associations…the majority cannot bind the minority." Adding insult to injury, the courts ordered Livingston to pay Lynch's legal bills. Legal wrangling over steamboats was just getting started.

The Modern Patent System Takes Shape

Another convoluted case involving Fulton's and Livingston's steamboat company was instrumental in clarifying the role of federal and state governments in issuing patents. Through national patents and state grants, Robert Fulton and Robert Livingston hoped to dominate the steamboat business in the United States. They teamed up with New Yorker and fellow inventor, Nicholas Roosevelt, to expand operations westward. But without the oversized political influence that Livingston possessed in New York, they were successful in getting a statewide monopoly only in Louisiana (where, apparently, Livingston's family connections to local politicians were a sizable factor).

Fulton tried to expand his reach by taking a broad and aggressive interpretation of their New York grant; any steamboat traffic that involved passage in New York waters was theirs to control, even for interstate routes. He had already expanded the initial New York City to Albany route with additional services between Manhattan and Brooklyn, and across the Long Island Sound to connect New York and Connecticut.

Aaron Ogden, a one-time governor of New Jersey, liked what he saw of Fulton's steamboat operations and decided to go into the steamboat business himself by ferrying passengers between New Jersey and New York. Fulton threatened legal action and Ogden capitulated by purchasing a license from Fulton in order to continue the new service. A bit later, with his partner Thomas Gibbons, Ogden expanded service between several New Jersey ports as well, using routes that took them through New York waters.

Fulton's company took the pair to court in New York, arguing that the expanded service was a violation of Fulton's exclusive patent rights and were not covered by the licensing arrangements made before the new routes were launched. In a somewhat tortured interpretation of both state and federal laws at the time, the court decided that Ogden's NJ-NY route was in keeping with the terms of the license agreement and could continue but imposed an injunction on the NJ-NJ routes managed by Gibbons as a violation of Fulton's monopoly.

As happens all too often, the partnership between Ogden and Gibbons took a bitter turn. The relationship between the two men disintegrated, and Gibbons, working with a young Cornelius Vanderbilt as his ship's captain, established a NY-NJ route in direct competition with Ogden's service. This led to further lawsuits, this time between Ogden and Gibbons, that worked their way through the New York courts. At each turn, Ogden's license for the interstate route was upheld and Gibbons was found to be in violation of the monopoly rights still held by Fulton. Not content with the state's decision, Gibbons took the matter to the Supreme Court, which overturned the state decisions in 1820, finding in favor of Gibbons and allowing him to continue his routes.

Gibbons v Ogden stands as one of the landmark legal decisions of the Supreme Court. It accepted the argument of Gibbon's lawyer, Daniel Webster, and asserted the complete authority of the federal government in matters of interstate commerce, pursuant to Article 1, Section 8 of the Constitution, which grants to Congress the power "To regulate Commerce with foreign Nations, and among the several States, and with the Indian

Tribes." The expansive interpretation of the interstate commerce clause championed by Chief Justice John Marshall and the Court has since become the basis for federal authorities in arenas as diverse as environmental law, national drug policy and civil rights.

Interestingly, the Supreme Court did not turn to the Constitution's patent language to assert federal exclusivity over the issuance of patents, a step which—had they taken it—would have invalidated state patents, such as New York's grant to Fulton and Livingston. But the impact of the decision on the patent system was pronounced, just the same. Even intrastate grants could be invalidated if they affected commerce between states. This was the case with the New York grant, since the boats moved mail, goods and passengers from many states, and the entire grant was eventually invalidated.

But clarity about who should issue patents for inventions did not do much to resolve patent ownership issues. By the 1830s, the US Patent Office was issuing about 1,000 patents each year without any assessment of a so-called invention's feasibility or originality. Applicants were visiting the Patent Office, reviewing drawings and models of already-patented inventions, copying these outright and requesting their own patent for the same item. Despite the Constitution's objective to "promote the progress of science and useful arts," the Patent Office had no discretion to refuse patents to applicants that offered neither progress or utility. Bureaucrats and inventors alike became increasingly frustrated with the issuance of insubstantial patents, the administrative burden they imposed on the senior government officials who signed off on them, and the proliferation of lawsuits that resulted.

A history of the Patent Office summed up the situation:

> The issuance of patents to pirates was a common occurrence, and indeed the Patent Office furnished every facility to aid them. Copies of models of previous inventions were made in the model rooms and used to demand patents for similar inventions next door in the Superintendent's Office. Even when an applicant was told that his invention was a direct copy of a previous invention, as had happened the previous week, he demanded and obtained his patent for the same invention. With the Great Seal and the signature of the President on his pirated patent, the pirate patentee could sell state, town and county rights all over the country to people who thought that the Great Seal and the signature of the President actually meant that the patent was valid. The present system provided a rich harvest for lawyers, but ruin for many an honest mechanic.

To make matters even worse, the fees collected by the Patent Office—which exceeded the costs of running the patent system—went to general Treasury funds and the office itself was vastly underfunded. To address these multiple issues, Congress passed the Patent Act of 1836, revamping the system and providing the core review and approval processes that continue to this day.

The creation of a more robust and effective federal patent system, on top of the realignment of authorities brought about by Gibbons v Ogden, crystalized the roles of the federal and state governments. Patents and corporations were, at last, entirely separated in concept as well as in practice. State patent grants became less frequent even as grants of incorporation were becoming ever more common. Corporations became a state affair, while patents would come to belong exclusively to the federal government.

Modern Patents, Modern Challenges

The patent system is meant to encourage the process of invention and technological advancement or, as described in the Constitution, "To promote the progress of science and useful arts". It seems to work that way at times (though, in truth, there's no way to know if technology would have advanced faster or slower in the absence of a patent system). But not always. Patents are no longer the purview solely of storied inventors like Edison and the Wright brothers. They have become a legal specialty and a business strategy in their own right, leading to practices that some critics consider patent abuse and a detriment to creative invention.

Patent trolls are a favorite target of the critics. Although the term is sometimes applied to the litigious mindset of some of the classic inventors (Edison and the Wrights among them), in modern usage, a patent troll is a business that has little to do with invention. Instead, trolls buy the rights to existing patents and then pursue an aggressive strategy of threatening (and often bringing) lawsuits against other businesses deemed to be infringing on the existing patent.

Protecting an inventor's exclusive rights to a patent is a legitimate undertaking, of course. But trolls are accused of taking advantage of a complex legal system to, in essence, extort money from hapless businesses seeking to avoid a lawsuit. This is especially so for small and medium sized businesses that can't afford the cost (or risk) of a long-term lawsuit:

by demanding a fee for the presumed infringement—a fee that is crafted to be less than the cost of defending itself in court—trolls are often paid to make their lawsuit threat "go away". But larger companies are targeted as well.

For example, a high-tech sounding firm named Blackbird Technologies was founded by a group of lawyers to acquire a broad set of patents that they used as the basis of suing more than 100 companies for infringement. One firm, Cloudflare, opted to fight back, even going so far as to offering a reward for information that would help invalidate Blackbird's patent holdings. Their fight was successful: a judge held that the patent Blackbird cited in their suit with Cloudflare was overly broad and overly vague. The patent, dealing with the automatic generation of error messages, "…"attempts to monopolize [an] abstract idea…", the judge wrote in finding the patent was invalid.

The Blackbird case is emblematic of another modern issue that has been the focus of much concern in the Information Age: software patents. Although we often think of patents as involving physical items like the telephone or airplane, the Information Age has ushered in new categories of invention that are far more intangible. Software is a legitimate invention, or at least, can be, in terms of meeting patent tests of novelty and usefulness. But software patents generally cover the concepts that underlie the programs rather than the explicit code. Thus, Amazon was able to prevent other prevent other online merchants from using "one-click" shopping unless licensing the option from Amazon. Google's "I'm feeling lucky" search option has also been the subject of extended patent disputes.

Bit by bit, legal systems in the United States, Europe and elsewhere are developing some rules of the road in terms of distinguishing legitimate from spurious software patents. The future of many patent portfolios, whether in major corporations or small "trolling" companies, will be strongly influenced by the rapidly-changing landscape of patent law.

CHAPTER 7

CORPORATE RIGHTS, CORPORATE POWER

In "The Measure of a Man", an episode of Star Trek: The Next Generation, the android character, Mr. Data, is threatened with, in essence, being turned off. Captain Picard comes to Data's defense, arguing that the android is a sentient being, entitled to rights and the protection of the law. It's a familiar theme in science fiction, having been explored in movies like I, Robot and Ex Machina: do artificial entities have fundamental rights?

Corporations are artificial entities as well but have never been faced with the fundamental question of whether, as an arbitrary creation of the law, corporations have rights. They do, by definition. Certain rights are built in to the very concept of what a corporation is: a right to protection of the law; a right to enter into contracts; a right to bring lawsuits. The characteristics we listed in Chapter 1 that describe corporations entail a number of legal rights that spring into being through the mere act of incorporation.

This is not to say that corporations have not struggled to keep—and expand—their rights. Far from it. The early "special charter" corporations sought to maximize the grants of authority their charters provided while minimizing obligations to the state. As charters became more boilerplate, corporate leaders found the limited set of rights granted unsuitable for doing business in the modern world. They advocated for more. Even as corporations came under the umbrella of an increasingly large, complex and intrusive regulatory scheme, as we outlined in Chapter 4, they campaigned for an expansion of corporate rights to give them greater legal authority to conduct their affairs. For the most part, their campaigns were extraordinarily successful. As new regulations created an increasing set of corporate obligations, laws and court rulings and changing practices were granting companies new rights and new authorities.

Figure 7-1: Demonstrators oppose expanding corporate rights

The transition from special charters to general charter authority was a shift in the most fundamental of all corporate rights: *the right to exist*. In the period of special charters, corporations had no such guaranteed right. A business could request a charter of incorporation, and could persuade, cajole and bribe its way into obtaining one, but there did not exist the assumption that the business had an absolute right to incorporation. Rights belonged to the king or queen or the legislature to grant a charter or not, as they saw fit.

The emergence of the general charter authority flipped that relationship around. A simple matter of paperwork would bring a corporation into being, no questions (or at least, very few questions) asked. Better yet, corporate existence was no longer chartered for short periods of years or decades; corporations became perpetual. Though not often cast in the language of rights and obligations, business gained the right to incorporate (and to live forever, if it could), and the state was saddled with the obligation to provide a workable mechanism for their existence.

Ted Nace's book, *Gangs of America*, offers up a thoughtful, colorful look at the historical accumulation of corporate rights. It is a decidedly US-centric history, for much the same reason as is our book: US corporations have been a dominant presence in the global economy since the 19th century. It also has a sharp focus on the negative aspects of corporate growth, but the author's views do not impinge on his careful scholarship. Nace divides his history into three overlapping periods:

1820-1900—laws creating new "quasi rights" for corporations
1886-1986[1]—rights created by judicial interpretation of the Constitution
1987-present—international trade agreements extending corporate rights

His list of corporate rights gained during each period is an interesting compilation (though we're not convinced there's anything *quasi* about what Nace labels quasi-rights). In addition to conventional rights, like limited liability and perpetual existence, the author identifies important rights gained by corporations in the 19th century.

The first is "virtual location". This is a reference to laws that unshackled corporations from any requirement to have its headquarters—or any operations at all—in the state of incorporation. In fact, corporations are not required to have any real physical presence, other than an in-state agent (usually a commercial service) who can act to receive legal notices, filings of lawsuits and so on. A functional corporation can be little more than a post office box This provision eventually freed companies from almost all geographic constraints on their operations, allowing them to operate at-will across state borders and in international markets as well. That companies can shop around for the most advantageous place to incorporate—whether it's in Delaware or the Cayman Islands—is a direct function of the right to virtual location.

The second is the right of 'indefinite entity" or, to put it more informally, "shape shifting". Corporate identify became perfectly malleable over time. Companies could expand into new business areas without restraint—an option not available during the period of special charters. Beyond that, companies could change organizationally at will—a new name, a new corporate structure, purchase of or investment in other firms, or the spin-off of existing operations. Joint ventures, trusts, holding companies, shell corporations and other complex forms of doing business (and of hiding one's business) were available to such entities. We saw already how both Aaron Burr's waterworks-cum-bank in the 1700's and the Pennsylvania

---

[1] Although Nace, in 2003, gave 1986 as the extent of this judicial period, subsequent court decisions make it clear that the judicial expansion of corporate rights continues well beyond the 1980s and into the present day.

Railroad in the 1800's used innovative shape shifting strategies to advance their corporate interests.

The Supreme Court Steps In

As we discussed in Chapter 3, the federal government of the United States did not assume an active role in chartering corporations, leaving such activity to the individual states. The one exception was banking. In 1791, at the urging of Alexander Hamilton and other like-minded individuals, Congress passed *An Act to Incorporate the Subscribers to the Bank of the United States*. The law brought into being the First Bank of the United States. The bank was responsible for a series of firsts: the first national enterprise in the U.S.; the first national charter issued by Congress; and the first corporate rights case to come before the Supreme Court.

The Constitution was silent on the matter of corporations so it certainly was not self-evident that Congress had the authority to issue a corporate charter, whether for a bank or for any other sort of enterprise. Some very distinguished early Americans, Thomas Jefferson and James Madison among them, held the opinion that Congress had no such authority. President Washington was initially leery of extending Congress' authority as well. Hamilton and his supporters argued the opposite: that the general law-making powers of Congress allowed it to do as it saw fit, provided there was no specific restriction on the activity. It was this view that carried the day, though politics being politics, it required the compromise of limiting the bank's charter to a fairly brief period of twenty years. Ultimately, even a skeptical President Washington was convinced, the bill was signed into law in 1791, and the First National Bank of the United States started up operations. Its headquarters were in Philadelphia and it expanded with branches in major cities, including New York, Boston, Baltimore, Norfolk, Charleston, New Orleans and Savannah.

Its branch operations were not always well-received. Georgia imposed a punishing tax on the Savannah branch's capital, with the threat of increasing taxes until the bank branch was no longer viable. The Bank questioned the legality of the tax and refused to pay, prompting Peter Deveaux, a tax collector for the state of Georgia to enter the bank with armed marshals to seize what he took to be the state's due. First National brought suit against Deveaux for trespassing in the hopes of regaining the seized funds and avoiding future incidents.

First National filed its case in federal court, thought to be friendlier to the Bank's case than the local state courts. Deveaux fired back by challenging the right of the corporation to be heard in federal court. The Bank's charter from Congress clearly gave it the right to bring suit (and to be sued) but was silent as to which courts would serve as the appropriate jurisdiction. The conflict raised the question: did the Bank, as a nationally chartered corporation, have the right to have its case heard in federal court?

The dispute ultimately came before the Supreme Court. Corporate rights came before the nation's highest court long before human rights. The National Bank case turned on the meaning of "corporation" and its status under a system of federal laws only recently created. As Chief Justice John Marshall noted in the Court's 1809 decision, a corporation:

> …is defined as a mere creature of the law, invisible, intangible, and incorporeal. Yet when we examine the subject further we find that corporations have been included within terms of description appropriated to real persons... for the general purposes and objects of a law, this invisible, incorporeal creature of the law may be considered as having corporeal qualities.

In other words, "corporations" and "persons" have legal meanings that overlap in a complex and somewhat muddy fashion, a matter the Supreme Court would return to time and again.

The First National Bank was ultimately successful in its quest, receiving a judgement from the Supreme Court in the Bank's favor. It can be said to have won the battle but not the war, as the corporation's charter expired in 1811, not long after the case was decided. Despite the Bank's apparent success in stabilizing the young country's economy and currency, opposition to a national bank still ran strong and the charter was not renewed. The United States remained without a national bank—and without any nationally chartered corporation—for several years until Congress created the Second National Bank in 1816. Again, the bank was granted a 20-year charter and again, the charter was not renewed when its term ended in 1836.

In a series of laws passed from 1862-1865, Congress created a new national banking system without an expiration date and gave the federal government the explicit and unambiguous authority to charter national banks. These laws created a two-tier banking system that laid the foundation of modern banking in the United States: national banks regulated by the newly-created Office of the Comptroller of Currency, and other banks largely regulated at the state level.

Taxation remained a point of contention. The banks, like the match industry, paid federal taxes through revenue stamps affixed to some transactions. States imposed additional taxes on the banks within their borders, making no distinction between state banks and national banks. This arrangement worked for a while, however begrudgingly, but as the tax burden increased, and as differences among the states grew more pronounced, the national banks grew increasingly resistant. They argued that high-tax states would put them at a competitive disadvantage with banks—national or otherwise—in states with lower taxes. Beyond that, as federally-chartered entities, the national banks continued to question the very legitimacy of being subject to state taxation in the first place.

The matter had been addressed in court in numerous cases. The Supreme Court, in its 1875 case, Farmers & Mechanics National Bank v Dearing, while not prohibiting state taxation all together, largely exempted national banks from the vagaries of local laws. The court, among other things, reaffirmed the findings of an earlier banking case, McCulloch v Maryland (1819), which established that state law could not interfere with valid functions of the national government.

More specifically, the national banks argued that they were being taxed differently, and more onerously, than were individual citizens or other businesses with similar financial holdings. For instance, individuals were allowed to exempt some of their capital from local property taxes; the banks were not. As with the Deveaux case, the matter of "incorporeal" corporations—the banks—being treated differently from real persons was a matter of concern to the courts. This is not to say that corporations and people were identical, or should be afforded exactly the same privileges, but the special status of the national banking system provided a multitude of rationales for protecting it from haphazard regulation by the states. With the federal banking laws on their side, the national banks had a series of legal victories that greatly reduced their tax burden.

No such laws protected the railroads. The burgeoning industry was subject to a variety of taxes, including levies on the vast property holdings that rail companies owned. A revision to California's state constitution in the late 1870s changed the property tax rules and prohibited railroads from deducting their mortgage debts from the overall value of their property, a deduction that was freely available to individual taxpayers. The Southern Pacific Railroad Company, incensed at the change, refused to pay its taxes.

San Mateo county didn't take the drastic measure of sending armed marshals to the bank to collect its due, but instead took the matter to court, suing the railroad for collection of the taxes. The case, joined by other counties, wended its way through the state courts. Eventually, the California Supreme Court decided in favor of the counties. Undeterred, the railroad continued the case in the federal courts and ultimately, before the Supreme Court, where it was known as Santa Clara County v. Southern Pacific Railroad.

The railroad offered up a novel defense for its refusal to pay taxes: that the equal protection provision of the 14th Amendment—passed just ten years earlier to grant former slaves equal protection of the law—also applied to corporations. California's tax code, by singling out railroads and denying them protections available to individuals, was in violation of the equal protection clause of the 14th amendment. The amendment's wording emphasizes that due process and equal protection are rights not just of citizens but of any person within a given jurisdiction, a point of law important to non-citizens such as visitors and immigrants. But do these rights extend to corporations? The railroads argued that it did.

The escapades of Roscoe Conkling, who represented the Southern Pacific Railroad before the Supreme Court, have been well documented. Conkling, a former Senator who helped draft the 14th Amendment, insisted the drafters intended to include corporations in its meaning, going so far as to produce an unpublished journal that, Conkling told the court, substantiated his claims. "There was just one small problem with Conkling's account," one author notes, "it was not true." Conkling's version of events seemed designed to force-fit corporations into the meaning of the Fourteenth Amendment.

The Supreme Court declined to consider the 14th amendment arguments, deciding the case in 1886 in favor of the railroad based on other, more mundane, considerations. But the question of whether corporations were covered by the equal protection clause did not vanish. A court-provided summary of the case includes this famous passage:

> The court does not wish to hear argument on the question whether the provision in the Fourteenth Amendment to the Constitution, which forbids a State to deny to any person within its jurisdiction the equal protection of

> the laws, applies to these corporations. We are all of the opinion that it does.

Elsewhere, also in the case summary, is the statement:

> The defendant Corporations are persons within the intent of the clause in section 1 of the Fourteenth Amendment to the Constitution of the United States, which forbids a state to deny to any person within its jurisdiction the equal protection of the laws.

In other words, the Supreme Court appeared to be declaring, unambiguously, that corporations were "persons" in the eyes of the law, at least as far as the 14th amendment is concerned. The issue is so self-evident that the Court does not even need to hear relevant arguments: the matter is settled. Corporations are entitled to the same Constitutional protections as afforded to the freed slaves and all other people in the United States.

Two points provide important perspective on the situation:

1. The summary language from in which these excerpts appear is not legally binding language as it summarizes, and provides context to, but is not a formal part of the Supreme Court's decision. The decision is written by the Justices. The summary is written by the court clerk.

2. The court clerk for the Santa Clara County v. Southern Pacific Railroad case was Bancroft Davis, a former president of the Newburgh and New York Railway.

The origins of this language, and its status in the law, have been discussed at great length by numerous authors. We will not rehash that discussion here, except to say that this important principle of law, affirming corporations as people, has origins that are at best, highly unusual and to some observers, outrageously suspect (a 2018 article for Atlantic magazine is titled: "'Corporations Are People' Is Built on an Incredible 19th-Century Lie".)

Corporations are “persons” in the eyes of the law. Though not a new concept, the principle that corporations could receive the same Constitutional protections as individuals was now enshrined in a decision of the Supreme Court. Despite the controversy over the origins and legal status of the clerk’s note, the underlying corporations-are-people principle has stood the test of time and is certainly regarded as settled law.

John Dewey, in a1926 Yale Law Journal article, *The Historic Background of Corporate Legal Personality*, makes the point that from a legal perspective, a corporation is perhaps best referred to as a "right-and-duty-bearing unit" but that, given the awkwardness of the phrase, "corporate person" is just an easier and more practical sort of reference. Dewey, and so many others before and after, make a reasonable point. "Person" can be given whatever meaning is appropriate to the situation, without necessarily being constrained by other meanings in other contexts. Just as we use the word "dry" to refer to a wine that is obviously wet, Dewey reminds us, we can use "person" to refer to a non-living corporation.

However, we can't help but wonder if the history of corporations would have unfolded differently if they were routinely referred to as right-and-duty-bearing units rather than as artificial persons. The Fourteenth Amendment, for instance, was adopted in 1868 to protect the rights of former slaves and includes the following passage:

> [No state shall] deprive any person of life, liberty, or property, without due process of law; nor deny to any person within its jurisdiction the equal protection of the laws.

Calling corporations "persons" makes the equation almost inevitable.

Had corporations historically been referred to by a legal term other than *persons*, it seems unlikely that the authors of the Fourteenth Amendment would have worded the amendment to explicitly include corporations within its scope, Conkling's "journal" notwithstanding. It's hard to envision an amendment intended to protect the rights of former slaves containing wording to prohibit states from depriving "*any person or right-and-duty-bearing-unit of life liberty or property without due process...*" It's only in hindsight that courts were asked to decide the extent of coverage for the word *person*. Given the usage in play, Constitutional rights began to increasingly align with corporate rights.

Pennsylvania Railroad and the Holding Company

Gangs of America, a work we mentioned earlier, tells the tale of Tom Scott, a little-known historical figure from a corporate era dominated by the growth of the railroad:

> The fact that Scott has been forgotten is not as striking as the fact the significance of his invention is scarcely recognized. .... More than any

> other person, Scott is responsible for the institution that has increasingly dominated the world since the late 1800s—the corporation in its modern incarnation.

To cut to the chase, Scott invented the holding company, a corporation with the chief purpose of owning a controlling interest in other companies. Tom Scott, as *Gangs* tells it, was the person, more than any other, who introduced the fundamental mechanism that made the holding company possible and brought the corporation into the modern age.

Thomas Scott would eventually rise to become president of the Pennsylvania Railroad later in his life. But he began his career with the railroad as a station agent in 1850, rose through the ranks to a superintendent in 1858 and rather quickly, to company Vice President in 1860. Along the way, he hired Andrew Carnegie as a telegraph operator, mentored him in the business and got him started on his first investments. Once he was well past his stationmaster days, Scott's duties for the corporation were largely political. He was, in essence, the chief lobbyist for the Pennsylvania Railroad.

PRR, as the railroad was commonly known received its initial charter from the state in 1846 and rapidly grew to substantial size. But Pennsylvania was still in the era of the restrictive special charter. PRR grew quickly as a company, but was stymied in its desire to expand its business both horizontally, by operating rail lines outside the state of Pennsylvania, and vertically, by combining mining, canal, river, timber and other operations that were integral to—but separate from—its rail business. PRR was hogtied by the constraints of the special charter system in which it operated and looked for a way to loosen the reins.

Scott's vision for the company was to consolidate and expand the patchwork of existing railroads into a coherent regional and, eventually, nationwide system. The challenge was particularly acute in the southern states, where rail lines were even more fragmented than in the north and the region was not inclined to welcome Yankee businesses in any ownership or management role of southern rail lines.

To work his way around some of the constraints PRR faced, Scott chartered a new company in Pennsylvania, The Overland Contract Company, managing to convince the legislature to provide a broad charter with no restrictions on the type of business the company could undertake. Scott was resurrecting (in all likelihood, unknowingly) Aaron Burr's trick from almost a century prior that gave rise to a major New York bank from a charter for a waterworks company—introduce vague and seemingly innocuous charter language that allowed a company to be much more than it seemed at first.

Scott's plan seemed to work for a while. He changed the company name to the Southern Railway Security Company and began buying up interests in small railways in the southern states. But after a few years of quiet activity, the southern rail companies became increasingly aware that something was afoot (a North Carolina newspaper warned, in 1873, "…"It is idle to shut our eyes to the plans of this Southern Security Company! We are almost totally in the grasp of the monster; its folds are around and upon us and are gradually being tightened..."). To counter opposition in the press, Scott used the flexibility of his holding company charters to buy up interests in local newspapers, thereby insuring positive press for PRR's endeavors.

The holding company was so integral to the railroad's strategy that PRR formed them by the dozen, sometimes chartering companies simply because a legislative opportunity presented itself, even though there was no particular plan to put it to use. PRR found them convenient to have on hand, just in case. "To this day", notes Albert Churella, a well-known historian of the railroad era, "it is not precisely clear how many holding companies [PRR] established". But, he adds, the Scott holding companies that *have* been identified share several characteristics:

> ... The charters listed "dummy" incorporators who were only tangentially associated with top PRR management. They included...Scott's private secretaries...Scott's name rarely appeared, for its inclusion would constitute an obvious signal of the PRR's involvement. ...the names of the holding companies did not include the word "railroad".

Scott deserves credit for his innovative use of holding companies, but like all inventions, the holding company had its predecessors. In 1823, the New York State legislature passed "*An Act to incorporate the New York and Schuylkill Coal Company*". The purpose of the act was "supplying the city of New York and its vicinity with coal" that was to be procured from the rich coal country along the Schuyulkill River in Pennsylvania. As pragmatic as the undertaking was, the mechanics of early-19th century charter law made the effort exceedingly difficult. When the Pennsylvania legislature voided the company's ability to carry out mining operations in the state—what authority did New York have, after all, to sanction business operations in Pennsylvania—the company directors formed a holding company, the "Forest Improvement Company" and incorporated the firm in Pennsylvania so they could continue managing operations from New York.

Tom Scott, whether first or not, certainly deserves attention for putting the holding company to effective use for what was then one of the most influential corporations in America. The beauty of the Southern Security Company was its status as a public corporation without public obligations—it could operate a railroad without being regulated like a railroad.

Holding companies came with serious flaws, not only in the business model itself, but in how powerful railroad executives manipulated politicians, newspapers, communities, competitors and other businesses to do the railroad's bidding. But the holding companies can also be seen as a necessary evil, or even simply necessary—a mechanism for getting the business of interstate nation-building done in a system designed in an earlier time for much more localized business activities.

Corporations Expand Their Rights

A few years after the Supreme Court decided the Santa Clara case, the court's decision in another railroad case, Chicago, Milwaukee & St. Paul Railway Company v. Minnesota (1890), extended a second clause of the Fourteenth Amendment—the right of due process—to corporations. Yet another railway case in 1893, Noble v. Union River Logging Railroad, pitted the federal government against Union River in a case involving federal authority to revoke an existing right of way. The Supreme Court ruled that corporations are also entitled to due process protection of the Fifth Amendment and the case was decided in the railroad's favor.

Not every high-level case about a corporation's constitutional rights was decided in favor of the corporation. In Hale v. Henkel (1906), a Sherman Antitrust case, the court affirmed the right of corporations to the protections of the Fourth Amendment against unreasonable search and seizure. But the same case also established important limits on constitutional protections offered to corporations for "pleading the Fifth". Although living individuals have a Constitutional protection against self-incrimination, the court found that this right, at least, does not extend to artificial beings. This limit on corporate rights has largely endured over the years even as other rights of corporations have dramatically expanded.

Following *Hale*, subsequent cases clarified that individual officers of a corporation could not invoke a personal right to plead the Fifth as a means of preventing the release of corporate records.

Numerous other cases made clear that corporations had other constitutional rights as well. Armour v. US (1908) extended to corporations the Sixth Amendment right to a jury trial in the jurisdiction where a crime occurred; a later case (Ross v Bernhard, 1970) similarly extended Seventh Amendment protections regarding civil trial to corporations. The Fifth Amendment protection against takings without "just compensation" was applied to corporations in Pennsylvania Coal v Mahon (1922), and protection against double jeopardy in Fong Foo v US (1962).

A 1976 Supreme Court case, Virginia State Pharmacy Board v. Virginia Citizens Consumer Council, was one of the first major tests of a corporation's right to the free speech protection under the First Amendment. The case challenged a Virginia rule that prohibited pharmacists from providing advertising information about the costs of prescription drugs. The justices ruled not only that such commercial speech is protected by the First Amendment, but that the right to commercial speech is just as much a protection for consumers (to receive such information) as it is for companies (to provide it).

The court further ruled on corporate speech in First National Bank of Boston v. Bellotti (1978), finding that company donations to support state ballot initiatives were a form of corporate political speech deserving of First Amendment protection. Pacific Gas & Electric v. Public Utilities Commission (1986), provided corporations First Amendment protections from so-called "negative speech". The case involved a rule requiring the power company to include with its monthly bills a message from a public interest group critical of the utility. But as the court's decision noted, "the choice to speak includes within it the choice of what not to say."

More recently, the Supreme Court's 2010 decision in Citizen United v Federal Election Commission—a case routinely labelled a 'landmark decision'—struck down some of the campaign finance rules that limited the ability of corporations (both profit and non-profit) to air certain political ads close to election time (the decision left in place, for the time being, limits on direct contributions to candidates). Corporations had been prohibited from making an "electioneering communication" (a political ad reaching 50,000 people or more) within a few months of elections or from funding ads advocating the election or defeat of particular candidates. The verdict in the Citizens United case struck down these provisions as unconstitutional, as a violation of a corporation's right to free speech.

Corporate Rights in the International Arena

The rights held by corporations are not defined solely by jurisprudence in the United States, of course. Each country answers in its own way the rights of corporations regarding speech, jury trials, private property, due process and other measures., Corporations in Hong Kong have essentially achieved the right to vote through representation on what are known as "functional constituencies" which are involved in Hong Kong's electoral process. The arrangement gives rise to the situation of an individual being able to vote more than once, as a person and as a corporate representative. Multiple corporate representations, in different topic areas and through various subsidiaries, give rise to outsized influence. One large Hong Kong company, the Sino Group, has been estimated to have the voting power of almost 16,000 citizens. A human rights group in Hong Kong challenged the legitimacy of the functional constituencies; the courts ruled that the practice is constitutional, but emphasized that its finding was not an endorsement of the wisdom of the practice.

Increasingly in our actively globalized economy, the international powers that corporations possess—and the limits to those powers—are coming to be defined by numerous bilateral and multi-lateral trade agreements. These agreements create a legislative framework that is outside of, and in some measure independent of, national legal frameworks. They are also crafted largely outside of the view of the public.

The extent and ultimate nature of the corporate powers conferred by these agreements is not always clear, as the often-imprecise language of the agreements has not yet been subject to much clarification by courts and international decision-making bodies like the World Trade Organization. A few such corporate rights are of note, however. Perhaps key amongst these is the "right of compensation" initially created under the North American Free Trade Agreement (NAFTA). Individual country laws generally provide for compensation to corporations for direct expropriation; if the government takes company land for a right of way, for instance, the company should be compensated at the fair market value for that land. NAFTA and other trade deals extend this corporate right of compensation to include indirect expropriation, a right that individual nations do not generally provide.

For example, if a country's environmental regulations prevent a foreign company from developing its land, the corporation may be eligible to receive compensation for the reduced value of the land, an option not available to domestic firms. While providing compensation may sound reasonable and fair in the abstract, in practice, the principle is most often used to challenge the environmental laws of a nation (or state or province) on the grounds that the rules are costing the company money. And because only foreign firms can invoke the international agreement, the rules have the effect of, say, a Mexican company challenging United States or Canadian sovereignty, or vice versa.

One of the earliest legal tests of the expanded corporate rights under international agreements like NAFTA came in 1997, when the government of Canada passed a law banning the gasoline additive MMT due to concerns about neurotoxicity. Ethyl Corporation, the U.S. manufacturer of MMT, filed a lawsuit against the government of Canada under the provisions of Chapter 11 of NAFTA, seeking damages for the loss of its market due to the regulation. The suit requested US$200 million. After a year of negotiation, the government agreed to withdraw the regulation completely and pay Ethyl around US$13 million to settle the case.

Dozens of other cases have been filed. Not all the filings have revolved around environmental regulations. Numerous NAFTA cases involve lumber import rules, "Buy American" restrictions, drug-enforcement restrictions on moving hemp products across borders, "mad cow" disease import restrictions, patent expiration decisions, trucking safety regulations, and many more. Similar cases—both environmental and otherwise—have arisen from other international agreements, such as the Central America Free Trade Agreement (CAFTA), a spin-off of NAFTA.

It's not the outcomes of these actions that are of interest as much as the fact that the lawsuits occurred in the first place. International treaties like NAFTA generally include provisions for tribunals, or other decision-making bodies, to convene to decide disputes between companies and countries. The decisions of the tribunals are binding (though appeals mechanisms do exist) and the courts—because they essentially are international courts untouched by any open-access provisions of national law—typically meet in private. Decisions can run into the millions or tens of millions of dollars and the mere threat of invoking a NAFTA tribunal can be enough to bring parties to the table and settle 'out of court' as it were. Relations become complex, as state and provincial governments can be pulled into disputes between corporations and nations. As the Ethyl MMT case demonstrated, the results can include the undoing of sovereign regulations.

With the dismantling of NAFTA—replaced in 2020 with the newly-negotiated US-Mexico-Canada Agreement—the status of these multinational compensation tribunals is up in the air. But this is not likely to be a corporate right that is surrendered lightly. The increasingly globalized nature of businesses, both large and small, is one among several key factors shaping the future of the corporate world, a topic we more fully explore in the next chapter.

CHAPTER 8

THE CORPORATE FUTURE

News story after news story tells of technological developments that will shape the future of human beings and the planet we inhabit. Amazon is experimenting with flying delivery drones. An Estonian company, Starship Technologies, is pilot testing rolling robots to deliver restaurant take-out orders. Ford, Tesla, Mercedes Benz, Toyota and other car companies are all perfecting the systems behind driverless vehicles, as are service companies like Uber and Lyft, along with information technology companies like Waymo and Nokia. About a dozen companies, SpaceX and Arianespace for instance, have launched private-sector rockets into space, with other corporations and consortiums entering the field. Hanson Robotics in Hong Kong makes startlingly realistic humanoid robots while Boston Robotics demonstrates parkour-capable machines that balance and leap with great finesse. Sex-partner robots are in the offing.

A host of companies produce ever-more realistic and more interactive video games. Modern movies are "filmed" as much on computer circuits as they are on studio stages. Artificially-intelligent computers that once struggled to play a highly-structured and rule-bound game like chess can now compete against—and defeat—champions in open-ended games like Go and Jeopardy, assist medical teams in diagnosing and treating a difficult cancer, and even tackle the improbable task of writing innovative software programs for other computers. Pharmaceutical firms are pioneering personalized medicines, therapeutic molecules customized for an individual patient's genetic code.

The makers of thousands of devices collectively known as the Internet of Things (IoT) promise a future that changes the lives of people at home, at play and at work. Already, many consumers can talk to their thermostats or televisions to issue simple commands or voice a query into the air (*What's the weather today?*) and have a unit from Amazon or Google provide the answer. Tiny security cameras and nanny cams not only monitor

Figure 8-1: The UN's sustainable development goals are one driver of corporate change

properties, but provide the homeowner the means to unlock doors, dim the lights, and respond to a knock at the door, even from thousands of miles away. Devices on cars and trucks can automatically pay tolls as vehicle passes a sensor, often (but not often enough!) without any need to slow down.

Beyond household and consumer impacts, IoT is in the process of upending and revolutionizing how business gets done. IoT merchants are promising an unparalleled boost in marketing and productivity along with an ability to manufacture products with a sophistication and level of detail that would have been impossible in decades past. IoT-enabled digital advertisements can already respond to individual consumers as they pass by, based on silent signals from a person's cell phone. Utilities rely on IoT to track power or water usage. Logistics companies track fleet movements and fuel consumption in real time. Manufacturers are turning to the 'smart factory' replete with IoT devices that monitor process conditions, track inventory, automate maintenance tasks and increasingly, handle manufacturing processes as well. Amazon (again) uses IoT-enable door locks to enter private homes (with permission, of course) to deliver packages and may deliver them to the trunk of your car as well.

Even something as fundamental as money is being altered, perhaps profoundly, by technological advancements. The development of Bitcoin, a form of cybercurrency, seemed a fringe and fairly whacky notion at the time it was first introduced in 2008. It was a decidedly non-corporate, non-governmental (almost anarchistic) approach to creating a new form of money and was embraced by a group of disaffected coders and libertarians sometimes lumped together under the category of *cypherpunks*. Despite its sketchy beginnings, Bitcoin, and its underlying technology known as a blockchain, has since gained a begrudging form of respectability and has the attention of the corporate world. We'll revisit it a bit later in this chapter.

Corporations are making these technologies or putting to use the ones they didn't make. They are being redefined by them as well. The corporate future will clearly be molded by robots, sensors, tracking tags, cameras, blockchains, and a multiplicity of flying and rolling vehicles, both earth-bound and in orbit—along with more distant technological advances like quantum computing, molecular manufacturing or laboratory-grown vital organs. But it's not just technological change that will remake the face of businesses. Many other factors are in play.

Future Globalization

Increasing globalization of the corporate world seems, at first glance, an inevitability. Even the smallest of companies can engage online with customers and suppliers in other countries. Improvements in transportation efficiencies (coupled with an extended period of unusually low energy prices) have made it economical to move products from port to port and city to city, irrespective of distance or national boundaries. Fiji Water, a popular brand of bottled water, actually comes from Fiji, yet it's cost-effective to ship it half way around the world for the benefit of thirsty, purity-conscious consumers in other lands. A trend towards international harmonization and multinational treaties has minimized many of the administrative obstacles for moving goods, services and money across borders.

Cross-border consistency was not always a priority, as any international traveler knows who has been faced with the challenge of plugging an electric device from home into the wall socket of a foreign country. Not only do the outlets differ in the shape and configuration of the plugs, but the amount of electricity delivered differs as well. Cross-border consistency was simply not a priority for most systems designed in the late 19th and early 20th centuries. Yet, modern electronic devices have achieved a surprising level of consistency—a USB port in Russia is compatible with a USB plug from Britain—thanks to the work of international standards-setting groups like the Internet Engineering Task Force. The internet itself works smoothly across national boundaries due to the adoption of globally-recognized protocols for its use.

Harmonization is not only a matter of technological standards. Rules for intellectual property—patents, copyright and trademark—were at one time wildly inconsistent from country to country, but have moved towards harmonization through the efforts of groups like the World Trade Organization and through treaties like the Berne Convention for the Protection of Literary and Artistic Works. Fairly obscure organizations (to the general public, at least) like the Society for Worldwide Interbank Financial Telecommunication, or SWIFT, have adopted rules and standards to facilitate the bank-to-bank transfer of funds around the world.

Other factors add to the momentum for increasing globalization. The sheer size of some modern corporations—we wrote about their comparison to national economies in Chapter 1—means their operations and customer base must necessarily spill over national boundaries as they are simply too large for a single nation to contain. McDonalds, which at one time proudly posted the number of hamburgers served worldwide, has since lost count and now merely brags about billions and billions of burgers. Coca-Cola's goal is to quench the thirst of pretty much every person on the planet. Company finances seem to burst the seams of national boundaries as well. The vagaries of national tax codes (a legal area unlikely to see significant harmonization) entice companies to rearrange their operations in order to take advantage of favorable corporate tax rates. The process, known as corporate inversion, has grown increasingly popular, although not without controversy: what some see as sensible tax minimization others view as unfair tax avoidance.

Even the mindset of the times can be said to foster greater globalization. The environmental movement has taught us that everything is connected to everything. We can email and Skype with someone across thousands of miles (almost) as easily as across the room. Workers move across some borders with relative ease, either through regional mechanisms like the Eurozone, worker visa programs that exist in many countries, or even the illegal-but-tolerated movement of workers across national borders.

Embodied in the phrase, *the World Wide Web*, is the modern sense of the interconnectedness of all people and the porosity of information as it moves from place to place with little regard for national origin or destination. Is it any wonder that companies increasingly view the world-as-a-whole as a potential market and as a source of supplies and labor?

But inevitabilities are rarely that, especially when they involve politics and policies and market preferences and innovations and a host of other variables that don't lend themselves to accurate prognostication. Even as the world seems to be barreling along towards unfettered harmonization in both the business and political spheres, disaffection with the impacts of globalization has emerged from disparate but increasingly vocal quarters. A grassroots movement against the institutions of globalization began in earnest in the 1990s. The Multilateral Agreement on Investment, a harmonization effort of the world's major financial nations that was spearheaded by the Organization of Economic Cooperation and Development in Paris, was in the works for years. A draft of the MAI was leaked in 1997 and by 1998 the entire initiative was scuttled. Activist groups were horrified at what they saw as a secret process designed to strengthen the hand of the world's wealthiest capitalists and corporations at the expense of the poor and powerless. This little-known and arcane international decision-making process became a rallying cry for a powerful grassroots movement.

Emboldened by their success in bringing the MAI to light and rallying opposition against it, protests extended to other agreements and institutions such as the "Battle of Seattle" protests against the World Trade Organization meeting in 1999. Large scale protests against international organizations like the World Bank, the International Monetary Fund, the European Council and the G8 Summit of World Leaders took place repeatedly: in 2000 in Washington DC; 2001 in Gothenburg, Sweden and Genoa, Italy; Rostock, Germany in 2007 and the Occupy Wall Street movement that began in 2011 and that Noam Chomsky referred to as "the first major public response to 30 years of class war".

It is not just political sentiment on the left that took issue with globalization. A wave of what is sometimes called nationalism or populism has emerged recently as a powerful factor in the political paths of several highly industrialized countries. Britain rejected its economic ties to the European Union in an infamous and surprising Brexit referendum in 2016. Citizens in other EU countries similarly advocated for a Frexit in

France and a Grexit in Greece, though these movements have not yet led to further departures.

Bernie Sanders and Donald Trump, running for President in the United States in 2016, found themselves the oddest of policy bedfellows. Both were highly critical of the North American Free Trade Agreement—NAFTA—a treaty they saw as doling out far too much power to multinational corporate interests to the detriment of American workers. Trump took his objections a step further, singling out individual companies for shuttering U.S. operations and moving to Mexico, and vowing to repatriate the lost jobs as part of his "America First" policy. One of Trump's first actions as President was to scuttle United States involvement in the Trans Pacific Partnership trade agreement and he later scuttled NAFTA as well. The 2017 impeachment of the President of South Korea, Park Geun-hye, centered on public outrage at influence peddling by major corporations like Samsung and Hyundai.

The populist sentiments on the left and the right are not solely focused on corporations, of course. Immigration, terrorism, national identity, public safety, government overreach and a host of other concerns are folded in as well. But the thread of anti-corporatism that harks back at least as far as Thomas Hobbes and Adam Smith is clearly an influence in modern day politics as well. Though the movement is diffuse and hard to define, it is motivated by a desire to lessen the power of big business and rein in the expansion of corporate rights.

The Return of the Corporate State

Globalization is also defined by a dramatic shift in the players on the world's corporate stage. Just as the concentration of corporate power moved from Europe in the 18th century to the United States in the 19th and 20th, it appears to be shifting once again in the 21st century. The United States still dominates in terms of the largest corporations but is increasingly finding that dominance challenged.

1984 Company	Country	Sales	2018 Company	Country	Sales
1 Exxon/Mobil	US	88.6	Walmart	US	500.3
2 Shell Oil	NL/UK	80.6	State Grid	China	348.9
3 General Motors	US	74.6	Sinopec	China	326.9
4 Mobil	US	54.6	CNP*	China	326.0
5 BP	UK	49.2	Shell Oil	NL/UK	311.9
6 Ford	US	44.4	Toyota	JP	256.2
7 IBM	US	40.2	Volkswagen	Ger	260.0
8 Texaco	US	40.1	BP	UK	244.6
9 DuPont	US	35.4	Exxon/Mobil	US	244.4
10 Amoco	US	27.6	Berk./Hath.	US	242.1

*China National Petroleum
Sales in billions shown as published, without adjusting for inflation

Table 8-1 Top Ten Corporations (from Fortune Magazine lists)

The shift away from the US and the emergence of corporations in Asia—especially China—is obvious even from this short list of the Top Ten companies. For the 100 largest companies, the US accounted for fully half the list in 1984 and a bit more than one-third in 2018. China had no entries on the 1984 list, but most recently accounted for 22 of the Top 100 corporations.

The emergence of China as an economic superpower has done more than alter the geography of the Global 500 lists. The three Chinese companies in the Top Ten are all owned by the government of China. Even companies considered fully private are presumed by many to be subject to the whims of the Chinese government, though concrete evidence of such influence is difficult to come by. The most notorious case is Huawei Technologies, #72 on the Global 500 list, and one of the world's premier manufacturers of cell phones and networking equipment. Several governments, the US and Australia among them, have restricted the use of Huawei equipment out of concerns that the company is so closely aligned with the Chinese government that their technology poses a security risk. The concern is not with already-identified risks (none have yet publicly come to light), but with the possibility that Huawei may be directed by the government at some future date to build hidden 'back doors" into its equipment.

Of course, all corporations are subject to influence from the governments under which they operate. But the emergence in China of large, multinational entities seen as indistinguishable from the government itself, combined with that country's pronounced lack of transparency, have heightened concerns that so-called private businesses are operating chiefly in the interests of Chinese nationalism. The government's international Belt and Road Initiative is a case in point. This multi-decade, multi-trillion dollar initiative is an attempt to rebuild the commercial infrastructure—roads, bridges, ports and the like—of dozens of countries throughout Asia, Africa, Europe and South America, linking their economies more directly to businesses in China. China sees the initiative as a means to "embrace a brighter future" while critics are concerned that China is using government policy and private funds to create onerous debt obligations and one-sided technological reliance on China's corporations for many years to come.

Chinese companies like Huawei and Belt and Road firms are not identical to the old trading firms like the British East India Company that also served as instruments of national policy. But nor are they very similar to how business has traditionally been conducted by large multinationals in the modern world. The way that current concerns are resolved in the international arena will shape the new nature of the corporation as China's odd hybrid brand of communism and capitalism plays an increasingly larger role in the world of business.

Sustainability

In 1998, Nike created a new executive position, the Vice President of Corporate Responsibility. The title was a nod to the growing importance of *corporate responsibility* as a social movement and an expectation among consumers. The job morphed over the years as those expectations, and the language underlying them, evolved. By 2009, the position was now the Vice President of Sustainable Business and Innovation and by 2014 Nike had changed it to, more simply and boldly, Chief Sustainability Officer.

Sustainability is itself a term and a concept that has morphed over the decades, harking back to the phrase "sustainable development" that was popularized in a 1987 United Nations' report, Our Common Future. Central to the notion of sustainability is the concept of intergenerational equity—the current generation has a responsibility to develop the world in a fashion that does not leave it worse off for our descendants. Sustainability is often visualized as a three-legged stool: we can best protect the future by paying attention in the present to environmental protection, economic empowerment and social equity. Subsequent work by the UN identified seventeen explicit sustainable development goals, ranging from "No Poverty" and "Zero Hunger" to "Affordable and Clean Energy" and "Decent Work and Economic Growth."

Translating the desirable-yet-vague goals of sustainability to specific corporate actions is a challenge that many corporations have embraced; about 85% of the S&P 500 firms publish sustainability reports on their company's commitments and progress. But it is certainly not a challenge that all corporations have accepted. We would paraphrase the attitude of the skeptics as: *It is the job of a nation's lawmakers to enact laws to protect the environment, provide justice for its workers and citizens, and build a flourishing economy. It's the corporation's job to obey the law while turning a profit.* In other words, obey the law, grow your business, and the future of the world will take care of itself.

It's a reasonable sentiment on its face. Laws, after all, are the codification of right and wrong behaviors that guide companies as well as individuals in their daily decisions. But for companies with a large consumer exposure and a sensitivity to brand reputation, obeying the law is often seen as the bare minimum. Society expects more and it is the job of the corporate world's growing crop of sustainability officers to make sure that more happens, and that a company's sustainability activities are well-documented and widely communicated.

The apparel industry, of which Nike is a part, has been particularly keen to appear responsive to sustainability concerns. The general business model of the industry relies greatly on contractor facilities to produce its products. Whereas General Motors or BMW manufacture automobiles in facilities they directly own, many familiar clothing brands do not do their own manufacturing. Nike's athletic shoes, Christian Dior's dresses, and Levi's jeans are all made by third-party suppliers under contract to the brand-name corporation. Companies have traditionally attended in great detail to the quality of products received from their supply chain, but paid far less (if any) attention to the actual conditions under which the products were being made.

Companies that are only tangentially in the apparel business, like Disney or various sports organizations, have historically paid little attention to conditions under which their branded items were manufactured. In this sort of "don't ask, don't tell" commercial environment, the presence in the contracting facilities of child labor, toxic chemicals, brutal sweatshops or unsafe workplaces generated little awareness on the part of the major corporations that hired the firms to produce clothing and footwear.

In the past few decades, the exploitation of workers, the environment and local communities in the garment supply chain have become a matter of pronounced and repeated concern. The activities of non-profit organizations and investigative reporters, combined with the speed and ease of global communication, has increased awareness of the connections between shoes on American or European feet and harsh conditions in factories in Haiti, Bangladesh, Thailand and elsewhere. Life Magazine published an expose in 1996 with the title, ""On the playgrounds of America, Every Kid's Goal is to Score: In Pakistan, Where children stitch soccer balls for Six Cents an hour, the goals is to Survive." The article prominently featured Nike soccer balls. Nike founder, Phil Knight, lamented in a 1998 speech that "the Nike product has become synonymous with slave wages, forced overtime, and arbitrary abuse."

The changing nature of the industry was well-captured in two quotes from a 2001 conference at the University of Illinois, "What's Behind the Label? Collegiate Licensing, the Apparel Industry and Sweatshop Issues." Todd McKean, the director of compliance for Nike, offered this observation:

> As a company, we certainly had our shortcomings…Our initial attitude was, 'Hey, we don't own the factories. We don't control what goes on there.' Quite frankly, that was a sort of irresponsible way to approach this. We had people there every day looking at quality. Clearly, we had leverage and responsibility with certain parts of the business, so why not others?

At the same meeting, Gregg Nebel, McKean's counterpart at Adidas, expounded on the limits of the oversight approach:

> We're not global cops. That's not our job. But we're in that position right now. Going out and just being the police in factories is not a sustainable function…We want to work long- term with the factories for them to take ownership of the situation…If we can get factories prepared, educated and oriented enough, they can control that and they can take that back to the people supplying them. We see that as a way to get farther back in the supply chain.

For well-known, brand-conscious companies like Nike and Adidas, the potential damage to their company reputation from repeated horror stories about conditions at their contractors and sub-contractors was enough to warrant a large-scale, corporate-wide response. The same is true for many other apparel companies, as well as companies in numerous other industries. Apple has taken heat for working conditions, and a rash of worker suicides, at Foxconn factories in China that make iPhones. The diamond industry has recoiled from charges of selling "blood diamonds"—gems unearthed at mines controlled by brutal warlords who use the income to fun their horrific activities. Food and cosmetic companies are reevaluating their use of palm oil as a result of criticism over widespread habitat destruction and slash and burn practices, endangering treasured populations like orangutans and contributing to global climate change.

Reading through the literature from groups like the Clean Clothes Campaign, it's clear that many non-corporate actors expect a future of ever-greater corporate transparency. Indeed, an earlier work of ours (*Missed Information*) proposed a novel mechanism for providing sustainability information for virtually every consumer item on the store shelves. Are these expectations realistic, though? Especially in an era marked by a persistent and deeply-held belief that corporations are already over-burdened with regulatory controls and societal expectations, will greater transparency become the norm? Or will the market witness a retrenchment to an older, more bounded way of doing business? One particular aspect of sustainability is particularly revealing of possible future directions.

Climate Change

Global climate change, although clearly fitting under the umbrella of "sustainability", may well be a 'prime mover' of the corporate future. Pretty much the entire global economy signed on to the 2015 Paris Agreements to slow the rise in greenhouse gas releases to the atmosphere (though the Trump administration has since backed out of the treaty, as a nation, the U.S. has continued to reduce its greenhouse emissions). Companies have, with varying degrees of commitment, pledged to reduce emissions. Fossil fuel companies are actively exploring energy alternatives, preparing for a time when oil and coal play a smaller role in the mix of energy products that power the world. The entire supply chain is impacted, as corporations push their first tier and second tier suppliers—right back to the primary raw material extraction stage—looking for opportunities to minimize greenhouse gas emissions. Corporations cast an eye in the other direction, as well, seeking strategies that will reduce the climate impact of products during their use and after they have reached the end of their useful life and are discarded.

Companies have been pressed to adopt greenhouse gas reduction goals. When Royal Dutch Shell announced a corporation-wide greenhouse gas goal—50% reduction in emissions by 2050—shareholders responded emphatically: that's not enough! Major shareholders, the Church of England among them, insisted on more aggressive, shorter term targets. Shell responded with a commitment to do exactly that (new targets are pending) and announced its intention to become the first energy company to link executive pay to meeting reduction targets.

Although there are numerous gases that contribute to the global climate change, corporate goals primarily focus on reducing emissions of carbon dioxide gas, which in turn means—at the very least—altering the mix of fossil fuels being burned for energy to favor sources with lower carbon emissions per BTU. But more to the point, it means moving away from fossil fuels as a company's principle energy source, and for the coal, oil and natural gases uses that remain, using these fuels more efficiently.

But the fuels that a company uses directly for, say, heating and cooling their facilities, powering industrial processes, and fueling the company's transportation fleet are only a part (and often, a fairly small part) of a company's greenhouse gas footprint. In the jargon of climate change, these are known as a Scope 1 emissions, the greenhouse gases that are the result of direct energy use. A second component, Scope 2, stems from a company's energy purchases. A facility that buys electricity from a coal-fired power plant is expected to account for some of resultant emissions, while a firm buying "green power" from a wind-generating power plant has smaller Scope 2 emissions to account for.

Perhaps the most substantial piece of a corporation's emissions profile, and the trickiest to account for, is its Scope 3 emissions—defined as emissions, other than Scope 2 purchased energy, "that are a consequence of the operations of an organization, but are not directly owned or controlled by the organization". Scope 3 emissions include a product's use: the consumer operation of a car, phone or lightbulb, for example, has its own greenhouse gas consequences, and these are included in the Scope 3 emissions of the company that produced the original product. Scope 3 also includes disposal practices, corporate leasing impacts, employee commuting, and even the greenhouse gas consequences of a company's investment decisions.

It is not unusual for Scope 3 to account for 90% or more of an organization's overall greenhouse gas emissions profile. Corporations with a serious commitment to reducing their greenhouse gas are faced with the substantial challenge of not only finding the means to lessen their direct emissions, but of working interactively all through a product's life cycle—with suppliers, merchants, consumers, waste handlers—to minimize climate change impacts.

Even firms that have not seen fit to make such a commitment still have to respond, in some measure, to the challenges presented by climate change. There's really no choice in the matter. McKinsey & Co., a corporate consulting firm, divides the corporate impact of climate change into two broad categories—value-chain risks and stakeholder risks—with three principle concerns in each category.

Risks in the value chain are focused in three areas: physical, prices and product. Physical disruptions are the impacts from the increase in extreme weather events that are a consequence of global climate change. Floods, droughts and violent storms threaten corporate facilities, interfere with transportation and disrupt the complex supply chain that underlies the global economy. The same disruptions pose price risks as well, as in the case of agricultural and industrial firms competing for fresh water in drought-stricken areas. Climate change puts certain products at risk: ski resorts may lose their snow pack; carbon-intensive fuel supplies like coal become less viable; specific chemicals may lose market share due to an outsized impact on climate change.

Stakeholder risks involve a corporation's relationship with external parties and falls into the areas of ratings risk, regulation risk and reputation risk. The first is the possibility that capital becomes more expensive for a firm due to the perception of climate-change-related liabilities. Regulation risk, as it sounds, refers to the complications that arise from government schemes to address climate change through regulation, whether financial (carbon tax or cap-and-trade plans) or prescriptive (emissions limits or fuel-use restrictions). The final category, reputation risk, involves how a company is perceived by pretty much anyone with an interest in the company's business: customers, clients, shareholders, journalists, government officials, insurers, financiers, and so on. A corporation that is not living up to its share of responsibility with respect to climate change, at least as far as its stakeholders are concerned, risks losing the good will of these external parties.

Of course, corporations have always been faced with the necessity of responding to external changes in the world around them. World War II turned car companies into tank and airplane manufacturers. Nationalization of oil companies in the Middle East shaped the trajectory of companies like British Petroleum and Standard Oil. The Great Depression in the 1930s and the Great Recession that began in earnest in 2008 forced many companies out of business and others to dramatically adjust their business strategies in order to stay afloat. New technologies compel firms to adapt or become irrelevant.

Wars and economic slumps come to an end. Nationalization has a limited impact. New technologies are quickly adopted as their advantages become clear. Climate change is a different sort of beast, however. The disruptions are geographically comprehensive, have no apparent end date, are predictably large-scale and at the same time, formidable in their complex unpredictability. Corporations that hope to operate into the middle and latter part of the 21st century will have no choice but to respond to the global-scale disruptions that climate change brings to the fore.

Inequality

The world, as it's always been, is divided into the haves and the have nots, but the sense that the disparity is only growing larger is the source of great deal of disaffection. Pronounced inequalities have been offered as an explanation (or at least, a contributing factor) for Brexit, terrorism, shareholder activism, a resurgence of the "strong man" politician, the Arab Spring, and even a decline in marriage rates. Joseph Stiglitz, writing in The Price of Inequality, describes the upheavals rooted in inequality this way: "Three themes resonated around the world: that markets weren't working the way they were supposed to, for they were obviously neither efficient nor stable; that the political system hadn't corrected the market failures; and that the economic and political systems are fundamentally unfair."

That’s a harsh judgement, and one which reasonable people might take issue with. But “taking issue” can also miss the key point: if enough people feel as Stigliz does, their frustrations will mount until change of one sort or another is inevitable. Whether increasing inequality is fact or perception, it's likely to be a significant agent of change for corporations doing business in the modern age.

In the corporate world, the issue of inequality has manifested most clearly around the topic of CEO pay. Part of the issue has to do with simple multipliers. When a CEO is compensated at a rate that is ten times the average pay of company workers, is that excessive? Fifty times? A hundred times? At some point, the difference strikes people as unfair, even obscene. A more complex part of the issue revolves around trends. People seem more accepting of great gaps in wealth if their own lot in life is improving. But it can seem the height of insolence for executive pay to increase year after year in times when worker pay is stagnant, job insecurity is on the rise, and worker benefits are becoming less and less generous. Are we in a new Gilded Age when a few exalted industrial families wallow in extreme wealth while the poor grow poorer and the middle class feels its prosperity slipping away? Or, as Bernie Sanders tweeted, "The Walton family makes more money in one minute than Walmart workers do in an entire year. This is what we mean when we talk about a rigged economy." It's a compelling issue, even when there is no clear cut dividing line between CEO compensation that is reasonable and compensation that is "too much".

From Stigliz again:

> Numbers on compensation of corporate executives…tell the story. We described earlier the huge gap between CEO pay and that of the typical worker—more than 200 times greater—a number markedly higher than in other countries (in Japan, for instance, the corresponding ratio is 16 to 1) and even markedly higher than it was in the United States a quarter century ago. The old U.S. ratio of 30 to 1 now seems quaint by comparison. It strains credulity to think that over the intervening years CEOs as a group have increased their productivity so much, relative to the average worker, that a multiple of more than 200 could be justified. Indeed, the available data on the success of U.S. companies provide no support for such a view

But the flip side of the conversation is compelling as well. Why shouldn't a CEO receive whatever combination of salary, bonuses, stock options and benefits that the corporate board sees fit to offer? If the movie star with millions of fans can command an exorbitant salary for the prospect of bringing millions of viewers to the movie theater, why shouldn't a company executive receive a similarly large (or larger) salary for the prospect of bringing in billions in new revenue? In neither case is performance guaranteed; both the star and the CEO are being paid for a belief in their potential to perform, a belief buttressed by past successes.

But flops do happen, and consistent failure to meet expectations will likely mean both superstars getting the boot. This is the marketplace at work; nothing more, nothing less. It was put this way by N. Gregory Mankiw, a Harvard economist, in his paper, Defending the One Percent: "…the most natural explanation of high CEO pay is that the value of a good CEO is extraordinarily high."

And that, of course, is a big part of the problem. If the subtext of the CEO's pay package is that "we greatly value what you do," the message going to the workers who are laid off, or denied salary increases or are watching their benefits disappear is the precise opposite: "we don't particularly value your contribution". Corporations that consistently communicate both those messages may, in the eyes of management and academic economists, simply be responding to market forces, offering vastly larger compensation to hard-to-replace senior managers than to workers deemed entirely fungible. But corporations that do so may be running a big risk. The tensions that result are not simply between bosses and workers. As William Vanderbilt's "the public be damned" comment (or historically less distant, Leona Helmsley's "only the little people pay taxes") reminds us, public perception factors into the equation as well.

At least partially in response to inequality issues, a few firms have adopted minimum wage scales that exceed those required by law. Amazon, for example, pays its U.S. employees at least $15 an hour, more than double the federal minimum wage of $7.25. When asked about the company's rationale, Jeff Bezos, said: "We listened to our critics, thought hard about what we wanted to do, and decided we want to lead…We're excited about this change and encourage our competitors and other large employers to join us."

There are other corporate dimensions to equity beyond just the distance between worker and executive salaries. It's been widely reported that, in the United States, there is a pay gap between men and women; female workers earning just 80% of their male counterparts for equivalent work in equivalent job titles. The gap is even larger for women of color. Similar disparities have been reported along other social dimensions such as race or immigrant status. Even if such pay gaps can be closed (or even, as some have argued, they are more an artifact of limited data rather than a genuine gap in pay scales) other types of disparities exist and are fairly unequivocal.

Witness the dearth of women or minorities in the pantheon of CEOs of large corporations or as members of corporate boards. In response, at least nine countries have passed laws requiring companies to step up their game in terms of gender equity. Belgium, France, Germany, Iceland, India, Israel, Italy, Norway and Spain require public corporations to improve gender parity on their corporate boards, ranging from India's and Israel's requirement of at least one female director to requirements in Norway and Finland of at least 40% representation. The Canadian province of Quebec has mandated an even split between men and women. Iceland has gone beyond board membership, requiring equal pay between the sexes and an audited "certificate of compliance" to document adherence to the law. In the U.S., California passed legislation in 2018 requiring public corporations headquartered in the state to include women on their board of directors and to report the gender ratio to the state. It is the first state to do so, and it remains to be seen whether the law passes legal challenges or whether similar measures are adopted in other states.

Decorporatization

Will corporations still exist a hundred years from now? Probably so. But the question strikes us as well worth asking. Corporations are not a given. That they have been central to the economic momentum of the past two centuries or so is beyond dispute. But—as financial analysts are so fond of reminding us—past performance is no guarantee of future results. There are forces at work that promise to reshape corporate activity, and we have described these in the preceding pages. But there are also forces at work challenging the very practice and the very idea of the corporation. Some of these can be labeled anti-corporate and stem from human frustration with harms, real or perceived, from the things corporations do and from the things they fail to do. Other factors have no attitude to speak of but are simply new ways of doing things—new technologies or new systems—that can undermine individual corporations, entire sectors and perhaps the very notion of the corporation.

Friedrich Hayek, whose work in monetary theory was awarded a Nobel Prize in Economics in 1974, published a treatise late in his career called *The Denationalization of Money*. In it, Hayek argued that there is no compelling reason for government to have a monopoly on issuing money, nor any reason to limit an economy to a single type of currency. Hayek advocated private-sector currencies that would compete against one another just as products and services do, and in so doing, produce a currency (or currencies) with maximal efficiency and with exactly the features consumers desired.

His idea went nowhere and his work was largely ignored. But four decades later, the emergence of Bitcoin, Ethereum and other so-called cryptocurrencies have breathed new life into the notion of a denationalized (and not incidentally, decorporatized) system of currency. Bitcoin was introduced to the world in 2008, at a time when the global financial system was imperiled; stocks, bonds and the worldwide housing market were crashing and major institutions like Lehman Brothers Bank, General Motors and AIG in the U.S. and the Royal Bank of Scotland and UBS in Europe either collapsed or were in danger of doing so. The Euro suffered financial contagion from struggling economies in Greece and elsewhere. Even the U.S. dollar was shaky and the country's credit rating was downgraded for the first time in memory.

The introduction of an alternative form of currency like Bitcoin, untethered to individual governments or giant corporations, seemed at first a crazy idea but with surprising quickness gained traction as a concept worthy of serious attention and, eventually, serious financial backing. Bitcoin futures are now traded in mainstream financial markets and bitcoin-based exchange traded funds (ETF) are on the horizon. Microsoft, JP Morgan Chase, Banco Santander, Intel and other firms have formed a consortium to explore the use of Ethereum—a blockchain-based system similar to Bitcoin, but with added capabilities—in mainstream corporate applications.

A modest investment in Bitcoin at the time it was announced was worth millions of dollars in less than a decade. Its future seems both unbounded and precarious: it can grow exponentially in utility and value, or can crash and disappear as just a footnote in the history of technology. At the time of this writing, the value of a single bitcoin had plunged precipitously from its all-time high only to regain considerable value, enough to buy about seven ounces of gold.

If Bitcoin can emerge, rapidly, as a potential alternative to traditional fiat currencies, could the same happen to the corporate form itself? Might a non-corporate way of doing business emerge as a serious possibility?

Cryptocurrency itself may be one of the factors that could break the mold. Erik Voorhees, one of the early Bitcoin champions, put it this way: "We're all working for Bitcoin, the meta-organization of Bitcoin. It's the first decentralized, open-source company. Each bitcoin is a share of the company. There's no one leading Bitcoin, but it ties us all together, and as Bitcoin benefits, we all do." Hyperbole, perhaps, but not a totally unrealistic picture of what cryptocurrencies like Bitcoin are designed to accomplish.

A decentralized, open-source company with no one in charge, no board of directors, no one who can be held liable. A "company" that is not a company, but that could conceivably pose a challenge to the likes of Western Union, Paypal and—if the Bitcoin true-believers have their way—even financial giants such as international banks and credit card companies. Nicolas Cary, founder of a Bitcoin company called Blockchain, described the untraditional, very uncorporate nature of his early operations: "We run an international business. We have no bank account. All of our employees are paid in Bitcoin, we pay our services in Bitcoin, and we don't have any need to operate with an existing financial network at all."

Bitcoin, and other cryptocurrencies (there are many!), is modeled as a distributed system. Thousands of computers around the world contribute processing power to the blockchain—the diffuse but powerful data-handling network that is central to managing the availability of Bitcoin and securing Bitcoin transactions. Anyone with a computer, anywhere in the world, can be a participant and be remunerated—with Bitcoin, of course—for their effort (at least in principle…in practice, equipment to "mine" Bitcoin is power-hungry and expensive, and generally out of reach of casual participants).

Several observers, such as Brian Eha, author of the bitcoin history, How Money Got Free, and Dan Morehead of Pantera Capital, have speculated about decorporatized (our term, not theirs) models to social media services, as alternatives to corporations like Facebook. A Facebook-like service—social chat, picture and video posting—that tied people together through a currency-based blockchain could distribute income to its millions of participants rather than to Mark Zuckerberg or to holders of Facebook stock. Each *Like* or *Share* would mean a cryptocurrency micropayment for the originator of the content. The blockchain could automatically post ads and manage the "company's" finances.

Facebook is exploring the launch of its own cybercurrency, Libra, to allow its billions of user to easily exchange money, perhaps with the intent of forestalling what Morehead refers to as a shift from an "extractive" to a "cooperative" model of running a business, one in which profits would be shared among the site's users by distributing cryptocurrency tokens—users would essentially own a piece of the company relative to the number of tokens amassed.

There is nothing unusual about a new technology or new business model having a disruptive effect on existing business. Digital photography signaled the decline of storied companies like Kodak and Polaroid; Amazon brought down Borders Books; Netflix undercut Blockbuster Video; Uber and Lyft are challenging established businesses like taxi companies and rental car businesses. Can disruption really be so widespread as to challenge the very notion of corporations? Already, cryptocurrency visionaries have coined (so to speak) the phrase *decentralized autonomous organization* (or sometimes, decentralized autonomous corporation) in reference to a new type of business entity barely recognizable as a corporation. A DAO relies on the blockchain technology to pretty much run itself. The business model, decision making tools, and transaction records are all encoded in the blockchain. Though more of a thought experiment than a reality, there's ample reason to suppose that some types of highly-structured businesses—buying and selling stocks, for example—would lend themselves to the DAO model in much the same way that structured games like chess can be played by computer without any human intervention.

Would a distributed DAO have a CEO? Shareholders? A charter? A headquarters? How would a disgruntled client bring a lawsuit against a DAO, when it has no real jurisdiction to speak of? It's not clear how these traditional corporate concepts would apply to such a diffuse entity....if they would apply at all.

Even a modest degree of distribution is confounding. Consumers experiencing computer problems are already familiar (frustratingly so) with hardware tech support services claiming the problem is the software, and the software help desk pointing the finger at the hardware—a painful side effect of a very modestly distributive business model. As the Internet of Things (IoT) expands, and our homes, workplaces and vehicles become collections of dozens if not hundreds of networked devices, which company takes responsibility for a system failure?

Distribution of corporate resources already poses legal challenges. When the U.S. Department of Justice subpoenaed Microsoft to see the emails of a suspected drug trafficker, Microsoft refused. The emails were stored on a server in Ireland and the company questioned U.S. jurisdiction. The case wound its way to the Supreme Court, and was eventually dropped when Congress passed a law specifically addressing the issue at hand. The 2018 law, Clarifying Lawful Overseas Use of Data Act (the CLOUD Act…get it?) required US companies to comply with data request subpoenas regardless of whether the data was held in the US or elsewhere. Is the CLOUD Act the last word in this? Requiring Microsoft to release the emails could put the company in noncompliance with Irish and European electronic privacy laws; indeed, Ireland had filed an amicus brief with the U.S courts in support of Microsoft, prior to the case being dropped. A headline in the Irish Times summed up the convoluted matter this way: *US action on Microsoft email case could devastate cloud computing.*

It's possible that the increasingly distributed, increasingly diffuse responsibilities on the part of corporations will necessitate a new sort of corporate model, something not yet envisioned to replace the familiar model of a multinational corporation with a clear national identity as a US, or French, or Japanese or Australian corporation.

Distributed systems can challenge traditional corporations in other ways. Local power generation using rooftop solar panels and small-scale community wind generators—combined with local storage capabilities in high-density batteries—may one day minimize the need for central power suppliers. The so-called CSA movement—community supported agriculture—is a grassroots effort to move the food supply away from the clutches of corporatized farming and food processing. Distributed, open-source software programs, often of impressive quality, offer alternatives to buying (or increasingly, subscribing) to programs from Microsoft, Adobe, and other providers. Distributed computing—making use of idle storage and processing capacity on millions of computers sitting on desks (and laps) around the world—may turn out to be a more effective model for business-in-the-cloud than today's massive server farms that supply the storage and processing needs of cloud computing.

Technology might redefine corporations in still other way. Ray Dalio, founder of Bridgewater Associates, the world's largest hedge fund, wants his company to continue operating according to his management philosophy even after he is gone from this world. To that end, Dalio has commissioned a team of experts in artificial intelligence to create an artificial intelligence system that could effectively run the company. When software does the hiring, makes investments decisions, and sets the strategic directions for the firm, is there a need for managers any longer? As the Wall Street Journal noted: "The role of many remaining humans at the firm wouldn't be to make individual choices but to design the criteria by which the system makes decisions, intervening when something isn't working…" When a computer system replaces senior managers and the board of directors, is a corporation still a corporation?

Society itself may come to an explicit decision that corporations have served their purpose and are no longer needed. Certainly, movements like Occupy Wall Street and organizations like Wikileaks and Anonymous are no friends to corporations. However much they may seem to occupy the fringes at present, their political prospects can certainly change in the decades ahead (Bitcoin itself is an example of how an idea way out on the fringes can became a mainstream force in the space of just a few years). A group calling itself POCLAD—Program on Corporations, Law and Democracy—champions the idea of returning to a more limited notion of corporate charters and using government authority to revoke charters when a corporation is not providing an explicit, defined benefit to society.

Corporate personhood, however rational a notion to a lawyer, is a concept that simply rubs many people the wrong way. Is it beyond the pale to suppose that a law or referendum might one day be thrust forward to end the rights granted to corporations, much as a referendum was able to undo Britain's connection to the European Union? The administration of President Trump is committed to what it calls the "deconstruction of the administrative state". It does not seem impossible that some political movement somewhere will similarly rise to authority with an avowed mission of deconstructing corporate authority.

Deconstructing Labor

In some respects, a once-powerful organizational entity—the labor union—already appears to be on a path of 'deconstruction', particularly in the United States. In 1945, 35% of American non-agricultural workers belonged to unions, a figure that held fairly constant until the mid-1950s. Since then, however, union membership has steadily declined at a precipitous rate so that, in 2016, only 6.4% of workers in the private sector were union members. Although percentages are higher among government workers, union membership in this sector is also in decline as unions are challenged on several fronts. Economics are a sizable factor as layoffs decrease union membership and globalization transfers some formerly unionized jobs to non-union locations. But ideology also plays an important role.

The National Labor Relations Act of 1935 was passed in the belief that unions were a healthy counterpoint to the power of corporations and should be legislatively encouraged. But subsequent amendments to the NLRA permitted individual states to opt out of the law's pro-union stance by adopting so-called Right to Work laws at the state level. More than half of US states have adopted such laws specifically intended to weaken the power held by organized labor. Indeed, there are those who argue that unions are fundamentally wrong and wouldn't mind seeing them disappear altogether. As an analyst from the Cato Institute noted, "Unions are going the way of the dinosaur in the U.S. private sector, which is a good thing for workers and businesses… If right-to-work laws extend to the 50 states, then private sector unions will be dead in America."

Though not as pronounced as in the United States, unions are in decline in much of the industrialized world. In OECD member countries, union membership has been cut in half between 1960 and 2014, from 34.7% to 16.7%. Membership in Canada and Scandinavian countries has held up well, but declines have been across the board elsewhere and particularly precipitous in Australia (from 50% to 15%), France (20% to 7%), and Holland (41% to 19%).

Unions, though weakened, have not been deunionized, so to speak. They still have a substantial and occasionally vibrant role to play as a counterbalance to the authority wielded by large employers in the private and public sectors. But nor is it ridiculous to speculate about unions "going the way of the dinosaur", particularly when powerful political and social factors are dedicated to this end and are buttressed by changes in the economic landscape. One is reminded, oddly enough, of Christianity. The hierarchical and corporatized Catholic Church was challenged by a much more decentralized movement of Protestantism. Neither model replaced the other as both exist in the modern world.

Is it any less far-fetched to suppose that decorporatization might take hold, augmenting or even replacing the corporate model of business? Might the corporate brontosauruses and T. rex's of today become fossilized remains, of interest only to econo-paleontologists of the next century? The possibility, though remote, is worth considering.

Of course, the reverse scenario is also possible, and some would say probable (and others, that it's already occurred). Corporations might become so powerful as to eclipse the authority of nations.

Corporate Superpowers

As every movie-goer knows, corporations are the bad guys. The bigger, the badder. Cyberdyne Systems, creator of Skynet, was the corporate protagonist in the Terminator movies. InGen Corp. unleashes dinosaurs on earth in Jurassic Park. Tyrell Corp. operates from a 700-story headquarters, manufacturing and hunting replicants in Blade Runner. RDA Corp. ravaged an idyllic alien world in Avatar. OmniCorp controlled Detroit in RoboCop. Even the children's cartoon, Lego Movie, features a mega-villain dubbed Lord Business. The list goes on. Corporations are portrayed as soulless and powerful…the true powers behind the puppet governments that they secretly manipulate.

The cinema focuses on powerful corporations in the (almost always dystopian) future. In the world beyond movie screens, we have to look to the past to find true corporate superpowers. The ultimate example is one of the world's oldest corporations, the British East India Company, chartered in 1600. At the peak of its power, in the early 1800's, the East India Company was the unquestioned ruler of most of India. It's been estimated that this single company accounted for half of the world's international trade. Its private army numbered at 260,000, about twice the size of the English army at the time. It had a substantial navy as well, composed of both merchant ships and war ships. The company flag (eerily similar to what would become the Stars and Stripes of the United States) was recognized around the world.

The East India Company mustered armies, fought wars, enacted laws, administered justice, levied taxes, conquered territory, minted currency, seized vessels, built infrastructure and commanded trade. It entered into treaties, such as the Treaty of Allahabad, in which the subjugated Mughal emperor in India was compelled to refer to the company directors as "…the high and mighty, the noblest of exalted nobles, the chief of illustrious warriors, our faithful servants and sincere well-wishers, worthy of our royal favours…" Through business, theft, conquest and treachery, the East India Company made many people wealthy and antagonized many more.

There are modern corporations that wouldn't mind seeing a revival of the British East India Company style of doing business. Erik Prince, a former U.S. Navy Seal, founded Blackwater, the private security firm that played a substantial role in the Iraq War, the hunt for Osama Bin Laden and in early U.S. operations in Afghanistan. Prince has ambitiously advocated for a more substantial role for private security forces—what some would call mercenaries, and what Prince refers to as a "contractor force". "We should fight with an East India Company model," Prince explained, advocating for a larger private role in Afghanistan.

Prince's line of reasoning was two-fold: private troops are cheaper, and a private military can operate with far looser "rules of engagement" than the lawyer-bound U.S. military. President Trump's administration gave serious consideration to privatizing its military operations in Afghanistan before apparently shelving the concept. Prince is still pursing the idea directly with the Afghanistani government, where he has numerous supporters. The country's president, though, is adamantly opposed to privatization of military activities, leading to speculation that Prince is quietly advocating for new leadership in Afghanistan, where he is a frequent presence.

The United States is not Erik Prince's only client. Through a number of corporate entities, Prince has assembled an 800-member force for the United Arab Emirates, and trained a 2000-strong force of Somalis in anti-piracy measures. Though there's no evidence of larger forces being involved, one can readily imagine such corporate efforts not only expanding in the years and decades ahead, but gaining a degree of operational independence that goes well beyond anything that exists today. It also seems quite plausible that a corporation with a sizable military of its own will not have the distinct national affiliation that was so characteristic of the East India Company. Prince's current corporate affiliation with Frontier Services Group is based in Hong Kong and has substantial backing from mainland China. When companies can go "charter shopping" across the globe for the most favorable incorporation conditions—whether for the purposes of securing funds, minimizing taxes, avoiding regulation, maximizing anonymity or all of the above—a sense of corporate allegiance to any individual nation becomes secondary.

Might a "contractor force", whether Prince's or some other company's, become a national or international power? With Afghanistan as a purely hypothetical example. we can imagine a scenario that unfolds in several steps. NATO or the United States engages a private security firm to create a substantial presence of security contractors and equipment in the country, as an adjunct to traditional military forces. Over time, the contractor force increases its presence as the conventional army is minimized. After a decade or so, the general public has largely forgotten about their one-time military commitment as the private forces become the only foreign forces of significance in the country. As US and NATO financial support for the operations dry up, the corporation turns to Afghanistan's own natural resources as a means of funding its ongoing activities, much as the British East India Company turned to India's natural wealth.

In time, there would no longer be any practical distinction between the corporation and the country. There are other conceivable pathways—such as Afghanistan turning directly to private armies in the face of NATO withdrawal—but the outcome would be the same: Afghanistan in the mid-21st century becomes what India was in the early 19th century—a nation under corporate ownership.

How realistic a scenario is this? The fact that the Trump administration, an administration particularly prone to experimenting with the unconventional, rejected Prince's suggestion of an expanded role for privatizing the military, suggests the concept may be too far afield to be embraced by militarized countries in the first world. But Prince's involvement in countries like Somalia also suggests there may be other opportunities for private control of nation-sized military operations and ultimately, private control of a nation.

A militarized path to corporate superpower is a possibility, however remote, but there are other means by which corporations might achieve superpower status. Although soldiers and weapon systems are the most muscular and visible means of exercising power—the RoboCop model of corporate power—more subtle options are also available to corporations. Money, information and political influence can be as effective as military strength and can all serve to put a large corporation in a position to match or exceed the power and authority of large nations.

Governments are generally wary of private (non-nationalized) corporations that grow so large that the company's survival becomes inextricably intertwined with a nation's economic wellbeing, and indeed, with the economic wellbeing of the world. The "too big to fail" corporations are generally banks and insurance companies—entities with intricate financial tentacles throughout the economy—though large manufacturers can also certainly fall under the too-big-to-fail umbrella. Eric Holder, when he was U.S. District Attorney under President Obama, complained of companies that were so vital to the nation's fiscal health that prosecutors were loath to prosecute financial crimes, a phenomenon that was quickly labeled "too big to jail".

For example, HSBC, Europe's largest bank, was fined $1.9 billion in the United States for egregious and deliberate violations of financial laws. The bank deliberately circumvented anti-money laundering requirements in order to handle funds from drug cartels and international terrorism organizations. The eventual fine, though substantial, was just a small fraction of the bank's overall profits and, through a "deferred prosecution agreement" reached with Holder's Department of Justice, no bank executives were threatened with jail time or even charged with crimes. Similarly, a federal judge rejected initial SEC settlements reached with Citigroup and Bank of America for a variety of financial shenanigans. The banks were allowed to pay modest fines without any admission of wrongdoing, a situation the judge labeled "half-baked justice, at best."

The HSBC, Citigroup and Bank of America settlements occurred at a time when the financial world was still reeling from the 2008 mortgage debt crises. Regulators, always reluctant to criminally prosecute executives of large firms for fear of undermining the banking community, were especially sensitive during this period. The government in the U.K. intervened in the HSBC case, fearing for the British and global economy should the senior bank executives wind up going to jail.

But—as the 2008 financial crises made so abundantly clear—so-called too-big-to-fail firms can suddenly collapse even without the threat of government prosecution. BlackRock Inc., the world's largest investment firm, has assets under management of more than $6 trillion. What would happen if BlackRock suddenly fell on hard times, as happened to companies like Bear Stearns and Lehmann Brothers? Would investors have access to their trillions? Would funds be frozen for weeks or months or longer? With a great diversity of investment vehicles in the Blackrock portfolio, there's no simple answer to those questions. Oversight of some funds could be switched to another management firm if BlackRock went belly up. Many of BlackRock's investment vehicles carry the stipulation: "Not FDIC Insured * No Bank Guarantee * May Lose Value". Even for funds that are insured, could FDIC deal with losses in the hundreds of billions should the need arise? Even if transfer of the entire $6 trillion to other management firms is feasible, the ensuing uncertainty from a sudden collapse of BlackRock would send financial shockwaves around the globe that could take years…decades…to recover from.

Corporations become intertwined with modern life in other ways as well. The revolution in communications made possible by internet-based firms has certainly expanded interactions between human beings, whether across the living room or across the planet. But those same services have also created new pathways for some of humankind's more insidious behaviors. It is now possible for mass-murders to "livestream" their activities in real time on platforms like Facebook and Twitter.

These same services have notoriously attracted sophisticated fake news posts meant to broadly influence public opinion. Russian state operatives are thought to have created hundreds of fake accounts on Facebook during the 2016 presidential election in the US with the aim of influencing the outcome in favor of Donald Trump; the false information was shared more than 340 million times. Similar charges have been made of Russian influence in European politics, such as Brexit and the presidential campaign in France. Facebook has eliminated thousands of accounts in response to concerns over its role in facilitating, however unintentionally, socially undesirable behaviors.

Even companies that are a moderate size, financially, can have an outsized impact on the world around them. As noted in Chapter 1, Equifax's 2017 revenue of around $3 billion wasn't large enough for the company to make the Fortune 500 list. Yet, Equifax is one of the "big three" credit monitoring firms in the U.S., and has a significant global footprint. The company's slogan is "Powering the World with Knowledge," and it's not an idle boast. They manage the credit records of "820 million consumers and more than 91 million businesses worldwide". Equifax's data breach in 2017 spilled the records of more 143 million Americans, including names, addresses, driver's license data and—most seriously—Social Security numbers. The breach involved well over half the adult population in the U.S.

As large as Equifax's database is, it pales next to the records held by internet giants, Google and Facebook which each have a clientele of from one to two billion users. The Chinese search engine, Baidu, is closing in on a billion users as well. When individual companies have a large portion of the world's population as clients and holds information on an even larger portion, perhaps they've already achieved the status of a superpower!

What, then, does the future hold for the corporate model of doing business? As Yogi Berra is thought to have said (though he probably didn't!): "It's tough to make predictions, especially about the future." (Yogi was mistaken: predictions are ridiculously easy…getting them right is the tough part).

IN CLOSING...

Humankind has organized itself over the millennia into a handful of institutions capable of operating at a very large-scale. Key amongst these are governments, churches, and corporations. None of these institutions are perfectly angelic and none of them are unredeemably evil. Nor should we expect them to be. Corporations—like governments, like organized religion—are composed of human beings who bring to them all the promise and all the foibles that humanity possesses. That was the case in the 16th century, as corporations were just coming into their own, and it is the case today.

Corporate goods and corporate bads will continue to touch the lives of billions, regardless of how the future of business unfolds. Corporate heroes and corporate villains will be with us, some in the spotlight and many operating behind the scenes. A few of the worst corporate actors will be brought to justice in some meaningful way and others will get off the hook. The consuming public will continue to be amazed and delighted at the innovations that come into our lives, even as we sometimes find ourselves appalled at what corporate greed and intransigence are doing to the world. Governments will impose new types of controls. Corporations will resist.

All of which is to say that the world will go on much as it has been. But as we hope we have made clear in the preceding pages, "business as usual" really means continual change and adaptation, especially when the business at hand *is* business, and when rules, technology, and societal expectations change, and change again and then change some more.

It's not an entirely comfortable state of affairs. When we mentioned to a colleague that we were working on a book about corporations—their past, their emergence as giants, and their possible future—he commented grimly: "The future? Corporations win!" Perhaps they will. And "winning" could mean the sort of heartless, dystopian future that movie-makers (and our colleague, apparently) envision.

But it doesn't have to mean that. All institutions, corporations included, are responsive to the demands and expectations of the communities in which they operate. Corporations are expected to not only live within the law, but to go beyond minimal requirements and actively help craft a future world that is superior to the current one.

If we collectively hold them to this expectation, then as corporations win, we all win.

References

The sources of information for each chapter are listed below, along with a series of works that informed our entire book.

Online links are provided for some works. Most of these have been shortened for convenience. There's no assurance the shortened links, or the underlying original links, will remain operational. Searching online for the document title names and authors will generally reveal additional information and alternative sources for the materials listed below.

Broad, Insightful Histories of the Development of the Corporate Form

Appleby, Joyce, The Relentless Revolution: A History of Capitalism, Norton, 2011

Fortune Magazine, Fortune 500 and Global 500 lists of largest companies, numerous years https://fortune.com/rankings/

Nace, Ted, Gangs of America, Berrett-Koehler Publishers, 2003 http://www.gangsofamerica.com/read.html

Winkler, Adam, We the Corporations, Liveright, 2018

Wright, Robert, Corporation Nation, U. Pennsylvania Press, 2013

Chapter 1: What is a Corporation?

Charter of the Dutch West India Company, 1621 https://tinyurl.com/ta9xkoz

Davis, Joseph, Essays in the Earlier History of American Corporations: Eighteenth century business corporations in the United States, Harvard U. Press, 1917 https://tinyurl.com/tsfck24

Eisenberg, Melvin, Corporations and Other Business Organizations, Foundation Press, 2011

Mayer, Carl, Personalizing the Impersonal: Corporations and the Bill of Rights, Hastings Law J., 1990 https://tinyurl.com/y8k6388u

Tarbell,Ida, The History of Standard Oil, McClure, Phillips and Co, 1905 https://tinyurl.com/wb4n88o

Chapter 2: The Age of Discovery and the Emergence of Corporations

Brenner, Robert, Merchants and Revolution: Commercial Change, Political Conflict, and London's Overseas Traders, 1550-1653, Verso, 2003

Gerson, Armand, Studies in the history of English commerce in the Tudor period: I. The organization and early history of the Muscovy company, Appleton and Co., 1912 https://tinyurl.com/uhv8m2w

Hakluyt, Richard, The principal navigations, voyages, traffiques and discoveries of the English nation, 1886 https://tinyurl.com/u3gjtlo

Pinkerton, John, A General Collection of the Best and Most Interesting Voyages and Travels, Volume 1, Longman, Hurst, Rees, and Orme, 1808 https://www.wdl.org/en/item/18540/

Sicard, Germain, The Origins of Corporations: The Mills of Toulouse in the Middle Ages, Yale U. Press, 2015 https://tinyurl.com/vbeuwxo

Chapter 3: From Uncommon to Commonplace

Annual Report of the American Historical Association, American Business Corporations Before 1789, 1903 https://tinyurl.com/wzdkh82

Arsht, Samuel, A history of Delaware Corporation Law, 1976 https://tinyurl.com/rkenuk8

Benedict, Michael and Winkler, John, The History of Ohio Law, Ohio U Press, 2004

Blackstone, William, Commentaries on the Laws of England, Clarendon Press, 1769 https://tinyurl.com/w9jw3kr

Butler, Henry, Nineteenth-Century Jurisdictional Competition in the Granting of Corporate Privileges, J of Legal Studies, 1985 https://www.jstor.org/stable/724319

Evans, George, Business Incorporations in the United States, 1800-1943, NBER, 1948 https://tinyurl.com/t2wzjnj

Fitzgerald, J.A., Legislative Manual of the State of New Jersey, 1911 https://tinyurl.com/tzu5rgy

Golden Speech of Queen Elizabeth to her last Parliament, 1601 https://tinyurl.com/we6cspp

Grandy, Christopher, New Jersey Corporate Chartermongering 1875-1929, Cambridge U Press, 1989 https://www.jstor.org/stable/2122510

J.P. Morgan website, Aaron Burr opens earliest predecessor firm https://tinyurl.com/rwvw2hy

Leibiger, Stuart, Founding Friendship: George Washington, James Madison, and the Creation of the American Republic, U. Virginia Press, 1999

Littlefield, Douglas, The Potomac Company: A Misadventure in Financing an Early American Internal Improvement Project, Cambridge U. Press, 1984 https://tinyurl.com/ty2ya3w

Mahoney, Joseph, Backsliding Convert: Woodrow Wilson and the "Seven Sisters", American Quarterly, 1966 https://www.jstor.org/stable/2711112

Murphy, Brian, "A very convenient instrument": The Manhattan Company, Aaron Burr, and the Election of 1800, 2008 https://tinyurl.com/t84dmr7

Smith, Adam, The Wealth of Nations, 1776/2002, Oxford https://lccn.loc.gov/2002564559

Sylla, Richard, and Robert E. Wright, Corporation Formation in the United States, 1790–1860: Law and Politics in Comparative Contexts, 2012, Working Paper, 2012.

Watson, David, The Constitution of the United States: Its History and Application, Callaghan, 1910

Chapter 4: Corporate Regulation

Coffey, Bentley et al, The Cumulative Cost of Regulations, George Mason U., 2016 https://tinyurl.com/wwl4k3u

Dempsey, Paul, The Rise and Fall of the Interstate Commerce Commission: The Tortuous Path From Regulation to Deregulation of America's Infrastructure, Marquette Law Review, 2012 https://tinyurl.com/u2hot8x

Marketwatch.com, Here's the staggering amount banks have been fined since the financial crisis, 2018 https://tinyurl.com/ycqvhdos

Percival, Robert, The History of Environmental Law, IUCN Academy, undated https://tinyurl.com/uous3de

SHRM.org, Sherman Anti Trust Act of 1890, 2016 https://tinyurl.com/w5tyuxd

Vachal, Kimberly, The Interstate Commerce Commission—Past and Present, N Dakota State U, 1993 https://tinyurl.com/udm5as2

Wolford, Ben, Everything you need to know about the "Right to be forgotten", GDPR.eu, undated https://tinyurl.com/vuwom6t

Chapter 5: Diamond Match

Crass, M., A History of the Match Industry, American Chemical Society, 1941 https://tinyurl.com/v2f26bb

Fleming, William, America's Match King: Ohio Columbus Barber, Barberton Historical Society, 1981

Gross, Linda, Matchmaker, Matchmaker, Patent My Match, Hagley Library, 2019 https://tinyurl.com/v22mmzd

Ohio History Central, Diamond Match Company, undated https://tinyurl.com/ulu9hpa

Prero, Mike, The Story of a Giant: Diamond Match Company, undated https://tinyurl.com/tfpuqvz

Chapter 6: Corporations and Patents

Bracha, Oren, The Commodification of Patents 1600-1836: How Patents Became Rights and Why We Should Care, 2004 https://tinyurl.com/quto5ry

Dobyns, Kenneth, The Patent Office Pony; A History of the Early Patent Office, Kirkland's Press, 1994 https://tinyurl.com/sm5knxc

Federico, P.J., Operation of the Patent Act of 1790, 1936 https://tinyurl.com/uwm2nje

Flexner, James, Steamboats Come True, Fordham U Press, 1993

Garrett, Wilbur and Garrett, Kenneth, George Washington's Patowmack Canal: Waterway That Led to the Constitution, National Geographic Magazine, June 1987

Hubert, Philip, Inventors: Men of Achievement, Scribners, 1896 https://tinyurl.com/r653zjw

Mountvernon.org, The Potomac Company https://tinyurl.com/w22wv47

New York State Dept. of Education, Steamboats on the Hudson: An American Saga, undated https://tinyurl.com/sxsubcy

Ochoa, Tyler and Rose, Mark, The Anti-Monopoly Origins of the Patent and Copyright Clause, 2002 https://tinyurl.com/wsftp2b

Chapter 7: Corporate Rights, Corporate Power

Dewey, John, The Historic Background of Corporate Legal Personality, Yale Law J, 1926

Nelson, Scott, Iron Confederacies: Southern Railways, Klan Violence, and Reconstruction, UNC Press, 2005 https://tinyurl.com/sega4w6

Public Citizen, Table Of Foreign Investor-State Cases and Claims Under Nafta and Other U.S. "Trade" Deals, 2018 https://tinyurl.com/wny6k3p
Reclaim Democracy, Corporate Personhood, undated https://tinyurl.com/9s8guce

Chapter 8: The Corporate Future

Clifford, Stephanie, Wal-Mart Is Being Pressed to Disclose How Global Suppliers Treat Workers, NY Times, 2011 https://tinyurl.com/seyhpl4
CNBC, California law will require women on corporate boards, 2018 https://tinyurl.com/yc3qsztn
CNN.com, Shell is first energy company to link executive pay and carbon emissions, 2018 https://tinyurl.com/yycpdjqh
Copeland, Robert and Hope, Bradley, The World's Largest Hedge Fund Is Building an Algorithmic Model From its Employees' Brains, Wall St Journal, 2016 https://tinyurl.com/mmylsb6
Eha, Brian, How Money Got Free: Bitcoin and the Fight for the Future of Finance, Simon and Schuster, 2017 https://tinyurl.com/sjulxln
GHGprotocol.org, Overview of GHG Protocol scopes and emissions across the value chain, undated https://tinyurl.com/tjstrwa
Heckel, Jodi, Companies say they monitor work conditions at factories, Champaign (IL) News Gazette, 2001
Kaufman, Ted, Why DOJ Deemed Bank Execs Too Big To Jail, Forbes, 2013 https://tinyurl.com/rxruu7l
Mashal, Mujib, As Afghanistan Frays, Blackwater Founder Erik Prince Is Everywhere, NY Times, 2018 https://tinyurl.com/ybad4y2z
Mayer, Gerald, Union Membership Trends, Cornell University, 2004 https://tinyurl.com/chlong
Protess, Ben, Judge Rakoff Says 2011 S.E.C. Deal With Citigroup Can Close, NY Times, 2014 https://tinyurl.com/vw9qnh4
Stiglitz, Joseph, The Price of Inequality, Norton, 2012
Visser, Jelle, ICTWSS: Database on Institutional Characteristics of Trade Unions, Wage Setting, State Intervention and Social Pacts in 55 countries between 1960 and 2018, U. of Amsterdam, 2019 https://tinyurl.com/qlpdw3m